C000271423

Venice

MICHELIN
Travel Publications

CONTENTS

Venice is a legendary city. She chose the waters of the lagoon for her regal existence of more than a thousand years, the same water that has saved her from the clutches of time and yet threatens her very being. She is a city of a multitude of moods and faces: lively and affectionate to the inhabitants that fill her streets with their chatter; on the verge of a painful farewell for those who prefer her in the tragic guise of *Death in Venice*. Each visitor to Venice takes away a highly personal impression of the city's essence. Discover the narrow alleyways and secret corners of this historic city, such as the quiet district around Sacca della Misericordia or the unhurried Campo di Gheto Novo; join the locals at the colourful fish market near the Rialto bridge ; enjoy a glass of wine or a cappuccino in one of the many backstreet cafés; admire the Gothic architecture of the palazzi along the Grand Canal or the splendid Renaissance paintings that adorn so many of the city's churches. Despite its popularity as a tourist destination, Venice cannot be likened either to an amusement park or to a museum; it is a living city, whose fragile beauty and romantic history succeed in transporting the visitor back in time. ■

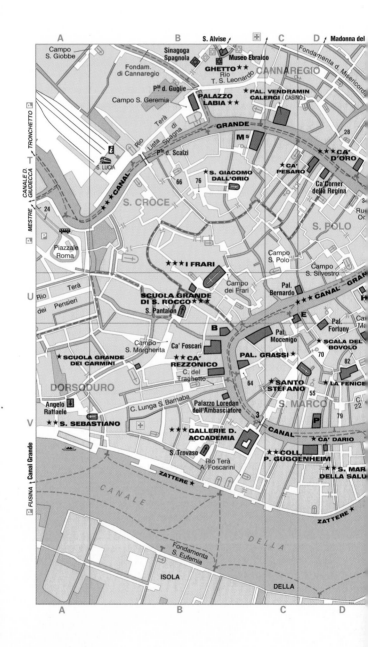

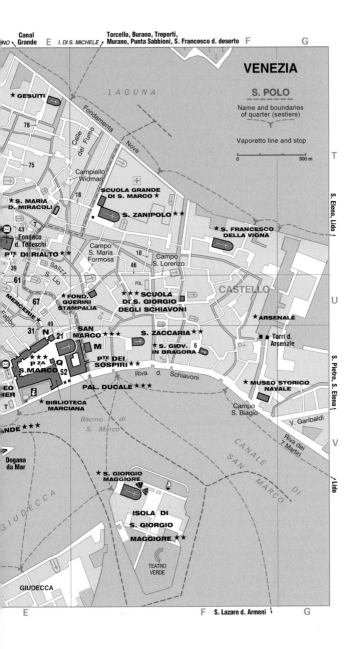

VENEZIA

S. POLO

Name and boundaries
of quarter (sestiere)

Vaporetto line and stop

0   300 m

LAGUNA

★ GESUITI

78

75

Fondamenta Nove

Calle del Fumo

Campiello Widman

18

★ S. MARIA D. MIRACOLI

SCUOLA GRANDE DI S. MARCO ★

★★ S. ZANIPOLO ★★

★ S. FRANCESCO DELLA VIGNA

43

Fondaco d. Tedeschi

P.TE DI RIALTO ★★

Salizz.

S. Lio

Campo S. Maria Formosa

10

Campo S. Lorenzo

46

39

61

MERCERIE

67

★ FOND. QUERINI STAMPALIA

★★★ SCUOLA DI S. GIORGIO DEGLI SCHIAVONI

POL.

CASTELLO

U

★ ARSENALE

Fabbri

31

49

N

21

SAN MARCO ★★★

M

S. ZACCARIA ★★

★ Torri d. Arsenale

★★★ P.ZA Q S.MARCO

52

P.TE DEI SOSPIRI ★★

★ S. GIOV. IN BRAGORA

6

EO MER

T

PAL. DUCALE ★★★

Riva d. Schiavoni

★ MUSEO STORICO NAVALE

★ BIBLIOTECA MARCIANA

Campo S. Biagio

V. Garibaldi

..NDE ★★★

Bacino di S. Marco

CANALE SAN MARCO DI

Riva dei 7 Martiri

Dogana da Mar

GIUDECCA

★ S. GIORGIO MAGGIORE

ISOLA DI S. GIORGIO MAGGIORE ★★

TEATRO VERDE

GIUDECCA

S. Elena, Lido

T

U

S. Pietro, S. Elena

Lido

V

Not to be missed

Fully experiencing Venice as the Venetians do means discovering it at your leisure; wandering through the campi and calli and listening to the musical local dialect all around you. But if time is at a premium, here are a few suggested "must sees":

Piazza San Marco★★★, with the Basilica★★★ and the Palazzo Ducale★★★

Gallerie dell'Accademia★★★

I Frari★★★

Scuola Grande di San Rocco★★★

Scuola di san Giorgio degli Schiavoni★★★

A vaporetto tour up and down the Canal Grande★★★

BACKGROUND

THE LAGOON

The Venetian Lagoon (the largest in Italy) extends over 550km²/ 213sq mi. It was formed at the end of the Ice Age by the convergence of rivers swollen by melted snow from the Alps and Apennines.

It provides a natural and complex habitat to flora and fauna between the Cavallino coast *(northeast)* and the Lido and Chioggia *(southwest)*. Water levels are maintained by the sea: its tides constitute both an ever-present threat to the Venetian Lagoon while also providing its regular safeguard from stagnation. The sea merges with the canals' fresh water through three channels (**bocche di porto**) by the Lido, at Chioggia and Malamocco, where dikes were installed during the 19C and 20C. The mainland reaches out a finger towards Venice, and the gap is spanned by the **Ponte della Libertà** (Bridge of Liberty). Otherwise, the coast's ominous profile cast in reflection across the lagoon is that of industrial developments at Mestre and Porto Marghera. Other buildings betray the affluence of tourism: the modern Tessera Airport and the prettified Jesolo beach.

■ The lagoon tide: life-blood and destroyer

Tidal changes occur every six hours, fluctuating between two high points per day. Low atmospheric pressure and the sirocco and bora winds are known to accentuate high tide, whereas high atmospheric pressure and north westerly winds tend to bring on a low tide. In this case, some of the rivers may dry up. Sea water is thereby drawn into the lagoon through the three ports, flushing "new" water in and "old" water out, assisted by a current from the rivers on the opposite side. Parts affected by these tides are therefore known as the **"living"** **lagoon**, whereas sections little affected by this lifeline are referred to as the **"dead" lagoon**.

1 Grey heron
2 Coot
3 Black-winged stilt
4 Cormorant
5 Kingfisher
6 Lille egret

The health of the lagoon is dependent upon the influx of "new" water brought by the tides. However, the inflow of fresh water has been greatly reduced as the rivers have progressively been diverted.

This has also reduced the strength of current across the lagoon and allowed vast quantities of polluting material to be deposited. In the 20C the problem has been exacerbated by the growth of industrial sites around Mestre and Porto Maghera. The reduction in oxygenated water flowing through the canals of Venice is gradually eroding the ability of plant and marine life to survive.

Quantities of macroalgae (ulva rigida) and insects (mosquitoes and the like) have increased at a fantastic rate.

■ Tidal flooding

The tide along these coasts can fluctuate wildly; for it to be classified as tidal flooding its level has to reach or exceed 1.10m/3ft 6in.

The last such occurrence happened in 1966 when consequences were felt way beyond the shores of Venice: the Arno overflowed in Florence, with tragic results. That year an alarming prediction said that Venice might possibly disappear.

Fortunately, radical action against further subsidence, including the closure of artesian wells on the mainland (1975), have proved the prophecy false.

Since the 17C the water level has dropped by 60cm/24in. In past centuries, once every five years, the tide would rise above the damp-proof foundations made of Istrian stone that were built to protect the houses against salt deposits. Nowadays, in the lower areas, they are immersed in water over 40 times a year and the buildings can do very little to stall the degradation process.

■ Venice, victim of the tides

On 4 November 1966 the mareograph at Punta della Salute registered an exceptionally high tide of 1.94m/6ft. Medium to high tides usually reach a level of around 70cm/28in, flooding the Piazza San Marco and, with a further 30cm/12in, even narrow alley streets would be inundated. Between December and February the city can be the scene of very low tides indeed, estimated at less than 90cm/36in. ■

4

5

6

THE VENETIANS

To describe the countless faces of Venice and ignore the particular personality of the citizens who live here would present a misleading picture of the city: it would sustain the unfortunate, commonly held view of the place as a museum or a monument to which a cursory visit is made.

To refute this, take a stroll down to Campo della Pescaria, visit the Cannaregio district, linger in a bar in Campo San Luca over a glass of wine, or idle away a moment on a bench in Campo San Giacomo dall'Orio to eavesdrop on a nearby conversation. Even doing the shopping around Sant'Elena will provide a glimpse of the living spirit of Venice.

As is the case with any other city, the best impressions of Venice are gleaned away from the obvious tourist areas.

■ The split personality of Venice

If setting out to explore the tourist's Venice, the way is clearly signed at every step by shopkeepers standing in doorways, enticing menus at a competitive "fixed price", corn-sellers proffering grain to attract the pigeons for that classic but kitsch photo ... This doubtless makes for one snapshot of Venice, but such a superficial veneer cannot do justice to the multiplicity of impressions to be gained. Every visitor must formulate their own individual opinion of Venice: it may be a highly personal response to the unique atmosphere of this enchanting city; it may be one tainted by bad weather. To stereotype the flavour of Venice would be detrimental to the magic of the place and offensive to her proud inhabitants.

ust outside the tourist mainstream, a local resident is often ready to regale the visitor with intriguing anecdotes; the long-serving employee at some magnificent *palazzo* will enjoy sharing its enthralling history with whoever gives him the chance; the parish priest, in his sacristy, is happy to unlock secret doors to hidden treasures in his custody.

Theirs is "the" Venetian personality too complex to be defined but too colourful to be ignored.

◼ Venetian idiosyncrasy

The Venetian is born with a **positive outlook on life** that is maintained by an imperturbable nature in which emotional involvement is tempered by a certain indifference to anything that lies beyond the lagoon. This leads them to a noticeably predisposed state of **tolerance**, an innate quality acquired from a knowledge of different peoples distilled over the centuries.

The blend of an almost Anglo-Saxon aplomb with boundless and all-embracing **curiosity** renders this personality even more fascinating.

Yet perhaps the attribute that most readily springs to mind is the pleasure the Venetian derives from **gossiping**, a pastime that delights all the more given the subtle sense of humour with which all Venetians are naturally and happily endowed, regardless of age, intellect or social class.

Jocular chatter is always conducted in dialect to allow quips and puns to sparkle and scintillate to full effect. It fills the bars and cafés, the shops and markets, but most of all the streets and squares, exchanged in passing or during a pause, which the Venetians take pleasure in granting themselves at every opportunity. Unlike citizens of other cities, Venetians are wholly sociable creatures, revelling in the advantages of sharing their environment with like-minded people who draw the calm and philosophical conclusion that only the truly essential priorities of life are worth worrying about, thus regarding the inconveniences of existence as relative. ◼

UNIQUE
TO VENICE...

To combat the waters, either too high or too low, and to make their way around the myriad islands, the Venetians built the gondola and hundreds of bridges; they also planted thousands of poles.

■ The gondola

No one knows exactly when the gondola was invented: the word *gundula* appears as early as 1094 in a decree of Doge Vitale Falier, although the reference relates to a massive boat equipped with a large crew of rowers – a far cry from the gondola we know today.

In the 14C, small boats covered with a central canopy bore metal decorations on the prow and stern. At the end of the century the vessel began to be made longer and lighter, the prow and stern were raised and the **felze** or cabin was added, affording shelter in bad weather.

From the 16C, boats were toned down by being painted black, a colour we might judge to be rather funereal, but in Venice red not black, is the colour of mourning. Today the gondola is about 11m/36ft long, 1.42m/4ft wide and comprises 280 pieces of wood.

The shipyards where gondolas are built and repaired are called **squeri**. At one time, each of these was allocated primarily to a family from Cadore, the wooden galleried constructions resembling alpine houses.

The **ferro**, a sabre-toothed projection placed at the prow and stern is the most crucial element of the gondola: implemented initially as a fender to safeguard against knocks

B. Juge, B. Morandi/MICHELIN

Paline, dame and bricole

Whether travelling by gondola, vaporetto or boat, there is always the risk of running aground. Navigable channels are identified by means of **bricole** – large poles (*pali*) roped together – whereas the entrance to a canal or a junction is indicated by **dame**, which are smaller poles than the *bricole*.

The **paline** are those thin individual poles that project from the water at odd intervals, to which private craft are tethered. They are evocative if painted with coloured swirling stripes, outside some fine building to mark the landing stage of a patrician family in days gone by.

today it serves as a counterweight to the gondoliere, and is used to align the boat around hazards in the narrowest passages. The curved fin is said to echo the dogal *corno* and to symbolise its power over the six **sestieri**. The tooth that "guards" the gondola itself is the Giudecca.

The **forcola** or rowlock, is an intricate piece of carving hewn from walnut, designed as a pivot that allows the oar maximum mobility.

The oar is made of well-seasoned beech.

■ The bridges

Among the hundreds of Venetian bridges crossed during the tussles of *su e zo per i ponti*, meaning "up and down the bridges", there are several like the Ponte Chiodo without railings or parapet, where rival factions such as the Castellani and Nicolotti faced each other during "fist fights". Projects for bridges with three arches met with less success.

Draining the rivers – Visitors acquainted with Venice will undoubtedly have witnessed a familiar scene in which the local authorities undertake to dry out the city rivers. This operation is aimed at cleansing the water and restoring the bridges. It is only then that it becomes apparent how deep the waters run and how hollowed out the river bed is. It is also extremely dark and malodorous since it tends to collect waste as well as any objects that fall into the water by accident.

HISTORICAL NOTES

Venice was founded in AD 811 by the inhabitants of Malamocco, near the Lido, fleeing from the Franks. They settled on the Rivo Alto, known today as the Rialto. In that year the first doge – a name derived from the Latin *dux* (leader) – Agnello Partecipazio, was elected and thus started the adventures of the Venetian Republic, known as La Serenissima, which lasted 1 000 years. In 828 the relics of St Mark the Evangelist were brought from Alexandria; he became the protector of the town.

■ The Venetian Empire

From the 9C to the 13C Venice grew steadily richer as it exploited its position between East and West. With its maritime and commercial power it conquered important markets in Istria and Dalmatia. The guile of Doge Dandolo and the assistance of the Crusaders helped the Venetians capture Constantinople in 1204. The spoils from the sack of Constantinople flowed to Venice, while trade in precious goods grew apace. **Marco Polo** (1254-1324) returned from China with fabulous riches. He related his amazing adventures in his *Boo of the Wonders of the World.*. Th 14C war with Venice's rival Geno ended in victory for the Venetian in 1381.

The first half of the 15C saw Vene tian power at its peak: the Turk were defeated at Gallipoli in 141 and the Venetians held the king doms of Morea, Cyprus and Can dia (Crete) in the Levant. In Ital from 1414 to 1428, they capture Verona, Vicenza, Padua, Udine, an then Brescia and Bergamo. The Adriatic became the Venetian Se from Corfu to the Po.

The capture of Constantinople by the Turks in 1453 started the deca The discovery of America cause a shift in the patterns of trade and Venice had to keep up an exhausting struggle with the Turks who were defeated in 1571 in the naval battle of **Lepanto**, in which the Venetians played an important part. Their decline, however, was confirmed in the 17C when the Turks captured Candia (Crete) after a 25-year siege.

The "Most Serene Republic" came to an end in 1797. Napoleon Bonaparte entered Venice and abolished a thousand year-old constitution.

y the Treaty of Campoformio, he eded the city to Austria. Venice and the Veneto were united with taly in 1866.

The government of the Republic was from its earliest days organised to avoid the rise to power of any one man. The role of doge was supervised by several councils: the Grand Council drew up the laws; the Senate was responsible for foreign affairs, and military and economic matters; the Council of Ten, responsible for security, kept a network of secret police and informers which created an atmosphere of mistrust but ensured control of all aspects of city life.

■ Venetian painting

The Venetian school of painting with its marked sensuality is characterised by the predominance of colour over draughtsmanship, and by an innate sense of light in hazy landscapes with blurred outlines. Art historians have often noted the contrast between the scholarly and idealistic art of the Florentines and the freer, more spontaneous work of the Venetians, which later influenced the Impressionists.

The real beginnings of Venetian painting are exemplified by the **Bellini** family: Jacopo, the father, and Gentile (1429-1507) and **Giovanni** (or **Giambellino**, 1432-1516), his sons. The latter, who was the younger son, was a profoundly spiritual artist and one of the first Renaissance artists to integrate

Lions' Mouths (bocca di leone)

E. Zane-MICHELIN

Lions's mouth
(Palazzo Ducale)

The "lions' mouths" or "mouths of truth" were found along streets or in the walls of public buildings. These masks were set with fierce expressions, the mouth carved hollow to accommodate anonymous denunciations posted to the State. These were taken into account only if two witnesses were cited.

1 Cushion capital Torcello (9-10C.)
2 Pluteus with peacocks Torcello Cathedral (11C)
3 Composite capital Torcello
4 Fretwork stone screen San Alipio door, St Mark's
5 Patera with Pascal lamb 6 Campanile di San Barnaba

landscape and figure compositions harmoniously. In parallel, their pupil **Carpaccio** (1455-1525) recorded Venetian life with his usual imagination and care for detail while **Giorgione** remained a major influence. His pupil, **Lorenzo Lotto,** was also influenced by the realism of Northern artists.

The Renaissance came to a glorious conclusion with three great artists: **Titian** (c 1490-1576) who painted dramatic scenes where dynamic movement is offset by light effects; Paolo **Veronese** (1528-88) whose sumptuous ornamentation and rich colours reflected the splendour of La Serenissima; and **Tintoretto** (1518-94), a visionary whose dramatic technique reflects an inner anxiety.

The artists of the 18C captured Venice and its peculiar light, grey-blue, iridescent and slightly misty: **Canaletto** (1697-1768) and his

The warm sound of music

Spontaneity and colour are also found in the musicians of Venice, of whom the best known is **Antonio Vivaldi** (1678-1741). Vivaldi was master of violin and viola at a hospice, Ospedale della Pietà, for many years, at a time when these charitable foundations were not only social institutions and orphanages but also academies of music and drama.

upil Bellotto (1720-80), were oth inspired by townscapes; rancesco **Guardi** (1712-93) ho painted in luminous touches; **ietro Longhi** (1702-58), the art-

5

st of intimate scenes; **Giovanni Battista (Giambattista) Tiepolo** 1696-1770), a master decorator vho painted frescoes with sacred nd secular scenes full of light nd movement. His son, Giovanni Domenico (1727-1804), adopted a imilar style. ■

R. Corbel/MICHELIN

6

A WINGED LION IN THE SQUARE AND THE PALAZZO

PIAZZA SAN MARCO

Every day, **St Mark's Square★★★** is the meeting place and destination for thousands of visitors. In summer and on special occasions such as the Carnival, there are so many people converging on the square that one might begin to doubt its attraction. It is advisable to avoid the "drawing room" of Venice at such times: the early hours of the morning and evening, the spring and autumn when the colours and the sounds are crisp and clear, are infinitely preferable. Each person's impression of St Mark's is unique, so much so that painters, photographers and writers have only ever managed to convey a snippet of the square's subtle, even sublime nature.

With the dawning of each day, St Mark's Square comes alive. Beyond the **columns of St Mark and St Theodore**, the gondolas and vaporettos come and go while noisy crowds gather around the hotly contested souvenir stalls. Almost every language can be heard as the tourists follow their tour guide's raised umbrella into the basilica or loiter under the porticoes, bewitched by windows of *passementerie* and sparkling jewellery and glass. Small groups of musicians play to the habitués of the legendary cafés, while vendors of bird feed continue to attract flocks of people and pigeons, by selling tokens of good luck.

R. Mattes-MICHELIN

The view from Piazza San Marco:
San Giorgio Maggiore

The centuries do not appear to have left their indellible mark on the square; however, if one could journey back through time, it would be just as busy in the 14C. The passing of the hours, since time immemorial, is still ceremoniously sounded by the Moors on the clock tower and the mighty bells of the campanile.

The vast trapezoidal space (176m/577ft in length, 82m/269ft maximum width) is enclosed on the north side by the **Procuratie Vecchie** and by the later 16C **Procuratie Nuove** opposite. In between, the neo-Classical Napoleon Wing or **Ala nuovissima** was built in accordance with the wishes of Emperor Bonaparte after the demolition in the early 1800s of the 16C Sansovino Church of San Geminiano.

In the arcaded portico of the Procuratie Vecchie is the **Caffè Quadri**, which was founded by Giorgio Quadri in 1775 to serve Turkish coffee.

Opposite, on the other side of the piazza, is the older **Caffè Florian**, also named after its first proprietor, Floriano Francesconi, which was opened in 1720. Its most renowned previous habitués have included the playwright **Carlo Goldoni** (1707-93) and the neo-Classical sculptor **Antonio Canova** (1757-1822).

The harmonious symphony of architecture, colour and light that epitomises Venice, even in the mind's eye of those who have never set foot in the place, is epitomised in the area which comprises St Mark's Square and the **Piazzetta**.

BASILICA DI SAN MARCO ★★★
(SAINT MARK'S BASILICA)

« *Pax tibi, Marce, evangelista meus. Hic requiescet corpus tuum*" (Peace unto you, Mark, my Evangelist. Here rests your body) is what the angel said to St Mark near the Rialto, as the Evangelist was journeying from Aquileia to Rome. Almost another 800 years were to elapse before the legendary prophecy was fulfilled, since when the symbol of St Mark has been synonymous with the Venetian flag.

■ History of the church

The first patron saint of Venice, San Teodoro, *Todaro* in dialect, was demoted by Saint Mark.

The vicissitudes of St Mark's relic, brought to Venice from Alexandria around the year 800 *(see box)*, were not yet over. After the fire of 976, which seriously damaged the church, all trace of the body was lost. Only three people knew where it had been buried and they took their secret to the grave. The inhabitants of the city were asked

The domes of
St Mark's Basilica

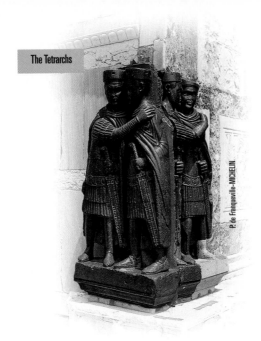

The Tetrarchs

P. de Franqueville-MICHELIN

to fast and pray for its return. The miracle then occurred: during the reign of Doge Vitale Falier (1084-96), on the occasion of the consecration of the third church to be erected on this site (25 June 1094), a part of a pilaster in the right transept crumbled to reveal a human arm. The sacred relic was removed to the crypt and later (19C) to below the high altar.

The 11C basilica is thought to have been designed by a Greek architect. It came to be the pride of the Venetians: Doge Domenico Selvo (1071-84) would ask merchants travelling to the East to bring back marble and stone pieces for its embellishment. This was how the mosaics in the domes and the vaults came about.

■ Visit

A unique spectacle at any hour of the day, it appeared as a "vision" to Ruskin. Silhouetted against the sky are the Basilica's five 13C Byzantine domes which culminate in a cross over the lantern. The lateral façades face onto **Piazzetta dei Leoncini** and Piazzetta San Marco.

The façade is pierced by five large doorways adorned with variegated marbles and sculptures. The central doorway has three arches adorned with Romanesque-Byzantine low reliefs, and above are copies of the four famous **bronze horses** (the originals are in the gallery of the basilica).

On the first arch on the left is depicted the Translation of the Body of St Mark.

According to legend

The second Evangelist was in Rome with St Peter, and following the Apostle's death **St Mark** became the Bishop of Alexandria in Egypt. In addition to the famous visitation near the Rialto that foretold the association of the name of the saint with Venice for ever after, there is a story that tells of another portentous adventure in Egypt around the year 800.

Two merchants set out for Alexandria with the intention of stealing the saint's body as the relics would bestow upon Venice the prestige it needed to "compete" with Rome or, at least, would affirm its politico-religious independence. This status was regularly reaffirmed by the Republic throughout its long history: even today, the city continues to enjoy the honorific title of Patriarchate.

So the body was taken in a chest aboard a Venetian vessel. The theft was organised down to the last detail: the cadaver was hidden under layers of pork to discourage any Muslim from examining the cargo too closely. The story is further endowed with a miracle, whereby the ship, venturing too close to some rocks, was saved when St Mark woke the captain in time.

On arrival in Venice, the precious relic was placed in the chapel of a castle belonging to Doge Giustiniano Partecipazio, subsequently consecrated in 832 as the first church dedicated to St Mark.

The south side abuts the Doges' Palace on the piazzetta. The first arch is framed by two columns surmounted with Romanesque griffins; the second arch contains the door to the Baptistry, framed with the **Acrean pillars (1)**, possibly brought here by Lorenzo Tiepolo from Acre in Israel as a trophy after the battle against the Genoese in 1258. Syrian in origin, two of the 6C columns have white marble shafts; the one nearest the piazzetta is of porphyry. This is the **pietra del bando**, from where laws would be announced. In 1902, when the campanile collapsed, this pedestal was damaged while protecting the corner of the Basilica. On the corner nearest the Palace

tand the famous 4C **Tetrarchs★**
2) or Moors – sometimes upheld
ɔ allude to the Emperors Diocle-
an, Maximilian, Valerian and Con-
tantine. They are otherwise said
ɔ be Saracens who, according
ɔ legend, were turned to stone
vhen trying to steal the treasure
f St Mark.

: is impossible to say what is most
triking about St Mark's. It may be
ne luminosity of this unique "tap-
stry" of mosaics which were first
xecuted in 1071 by artists brought
ɔ Venice from Constantinople. It
ould be the Eastern aura or the
2C pavement decorated with
nimal and geometrical motifs; its
neven surface caused by subsid-
nce only serves to heighten the
ensation of having being inherited
rom a mysterious and sacred past.
ntry is through the **atrium**.
)ecked with mosaics that relate
tories from the Old Testament,
hese herald others inside the
hurch that illustrate incidents
rom the New Testament. As a
vhole the mosaics transform the
hurch into "a great Book of Com-
non Prayer".

Mosaics★★★ – The lower part of
the walls depict the saints, the
middle section is reserved for
the Apostles and the domes are
dedicated to the Creator. The key
to each story is held in the dome
of the apse from where the story
unfolds chronologically. Christ as
Pantocrator towers over the four
patrons of Venice, with the area
above the atrium given over to the
Last Judgement. These last mosaics
are also the most recent, dating as
they do from the 16C.

The entrance door depicts the
Deesis, the Saviour in benediction
between the Virgin and St Mark.

The atrium gives access to the
Galleria e Museo marciano
which displays the **gilded bronze
horses★★**.

Of particular interest are:

**The Creation according to
Genesis (3)** – These are the oldest
mosaics in the atrium: in three concentric circles, in an anticlockwise
direction, they tell the story of
Genesis, beginning with the dove,
the smallest mosaic, to the east.

The **Arch of Noah (4)** depicts the
story of Noah and the Flood: no-

G. Targat-MICHELIN

BASILICA DI S. MARCO

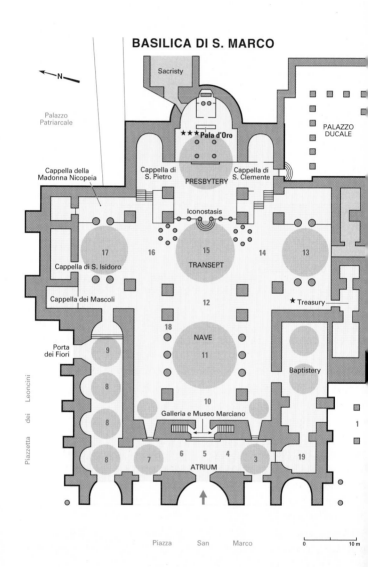

The bells of San Marco

There are five deeply sonorous bells, each with its own name:

La Marangona, the largest of the bells, was salvaged when the tower fell. Its name derives from the fact that it tolled the working hours of the *marangoni* or carpenters. It also heralded times when the Major Council met; the second strike, known as *la Trottiera*, acted as a signal for the nobles to 'trot' quickly over to the palace.

La Nona (the grandmother) rang at noon; *la Mezza Terza* (Middle Third) or *Pregadi Bell* was a sign that the Senate was in session; the notorious knell of the *Renghiera* or *Bad One* marked an execution.

ice the ark's little window during he deluge.

The **Arch of Paradise (5)** is by intoretto (1518-94) and Aliense 1556-1629) The Cross, Paradise nd Hell are represented as symbols that break with the narrative of the Old Testament stories illustrated previously. Before passing hrough the doorway, note St Mark n Ecstasy based on a cartoon by **Titian** (1490-1576).

The **Tower of Babel (6)**, a prelude o the division of the human race.

The **Story of Abraham (7)**.

The **Story of Joseph (8)**. In order o portray a person who is dreaming – in this case the Pharaoh – the mosaic artists resorted to a sort of bubble that unfurls.

The **Story of Moses (9)**.

The **Arch of the Apocalypse (10)** illustrates the visions described in the Gospel of St John. The dome nearest the doorway is dedicated to the **Pentecost (11)**.

The **West Arch (12)** presents a synthesis of the *Passion* and *Death of Christ.*

The **Dome of St Leonard (13)** or the Saints of the Sacrament, is decorated with 13C mosaics representing St Nicholas, St Clement, St Blaise and St Leonard.

The **South Arch (14)** has Byzantine mosaics which depict the *Temptations of Christ* and *His Entry into Jerusalem*, the *Last Supper* and the *Washing of the Feet.*

The **Dome of the Ascension (15)**. This encapsulates the most important moments in the story of the Salvation.

The **mosaics on the North Arch (16)** designed by Tintoretto.

The **Dome of St John the Evangelist (17)**. The 13C mosaics reproduce a Greek cross with biblical verses on the *Sermon on the Mount* and episodes from the Life of St John the Evangelist.

Continue along the left aisle. In the north aisle is the **Capital of the Crucifixion (18)**, a white and black marble structure with a pyramidal roof surmounted by an agate.

An **iconostasis** separates the raised presbytery (sanctuary) from the nave. Eight columns support an architrave bearing figures of the Apostles, the Madonna and St John the Baptist by Dalle Masegne (14C-15C). Beyond, a ciborium raised on **alabaster columns★★** precedes the **Pala d'Oro★★★** (Golden Altarpiece), a masterpiece of Gothic art dating from the early 10C. The relics of St Mark rest under the high altar.

In the Chapel of the Madonna Nicopeia is a venerated image of the Madonna and Child, called *Nicopeia* (the Bringer of Victory or Leader), because she served as the standard of the Byzantine army. Coming from Constantinople, the figure may have been brought t Venice as booty from the Fourt Crusade.

The south transept gives acces to the **treasury★** which contain a collection of religious object and ornaments which came int Venice's possession after the con quest of Constantinople (1204 In the **Baptistery** (*Battistero*) the famous panel which show *Salome Dancing before Herod.* Th baptismal font is by Sansovin (1486-1570), who is buried her in front of the altar.

■ Il campanile★★

The bell tower (99m/325ft high which dominates the square the symbol of Venice. It is a caref reconstruction of the 15C cam panile which collapsed in 1902 The **panorama★★** from the to extends from the Guidecca Cana to the Grand Canal across a se of roofs and beyond, to the island in the lagoon.

At the base of the campanile is th **Loggetta Sansoviniana**; statue of Minerva, Apollo, Mercury an Peace adorn the niches. The ter race is enclosed by a balustrad punctuated by a 17C gate. ■

PALAZZO DUCALE***

The palace was a symbol of Venetian power and glory, and was the residence of the doges and the seat of government and the law courts as well as being a prison. It was built in the 12C but was transformed between the end of the 13C and the 16C.

A pretty, geometric pattern in white and pink marble lends great charm to the two **façades**. The groups at the corners of the palace represent, from left to right, the *Judgement of Solomon* (probably by Bartolomeo Bon), Adam and Eve, and *Noah's Drunkenness* (14C-15C Gothic sculptures). The small loggia on the first floor is a delicate structure with quatrefoil motifs. The main entrance is the **Porta della Carta**★★, so called perhaps because of the scribes who worked there or the archives kept inside. It is in the Flamboyant-Gothic style (1442) and has on its tympanum a Lion of St Mark before which kneels Doge Foscari (19C copy). The gateway leads into the Porticato Foscari; directly opposite is the **Scala dei Giganti** (Giants' Staircase) dominated by statues of Mars and Neptune by Sansovino.

■ **Visit**

Start at the top of Sansovino's **Scala d'Oro** (Golden Staircase) and pass through a suite of rooms as follows: the Sala delle Quattro Porte (Room of the Four Doors) where the ambassadors waited for their audience with the doge; an antechamber, the Sala dell'Antecollegio, for diplomatic missions and delegations; the Sala del Collegio where the doge presided over meetings; the Senate Chamber,

The engraved story

The narrative function of the mosaics inside the basilica is transposed here onto the sculptural iconography that adorns the capitals, the corners of the *palazzo* and its pillars. Decorating the palace are allegorical figures representing the Vices and Virtues, Labours of the month, the Ages of Man and Signs of the Zodiac – all charged with moral significance.

Ponte dei Sospiri

Sala del Senato or *"dei Pregadi"*, where the members of the Senate submitted their written request to participate in the meetings. The Sala del Consiglio dei Dieci (Chamber of the Council of Ten) is where met the powerful magistrates who used the secret police and spies to safeguard the institutions. Beyond the Sala della Bussola, the waiting-room for those awaiting interrogation and the armoury (*Armeria*) is the **Sala del Maggior Consiglio** (Grand Council Chamber). In this vast room (1 300m^2 – 14 000sq ft) sat the legislative body which appointed all public officials; here also was conducted the constitutional election of the new doge. In the chamber hang paintings and portraits of 76 doges as well as Tintoretto's *Paradise*. Proceed to the Sala dello Scrutinio (Ballot Chamber) where the counting of the votes took place; the **Prigione Nuove** (new prisons) and the Bridge of Sighs. Further along

are the Censors' Chamber *(Sala dei Censori),* the seat of the judiciary and the Sala dell'Avogaria (*avogadori* were lawyers appointed by the state whose duty was to ensure that the law was obeyed.

■ A tour through the labyrinthine palace corridors

The magistratures that had seats in the palace operated in an environment that was anything but ostentatious.

Many of the activities, most of which were secret, took place in very restricted surroundings just off the grand chambers. Linked by a maze of hidden stairs and passageways, these still exude an air of mystery.

Although his office was small, the Grand Chancellor, the director of the Secret Chancellery (Venice's general archives), enjoyed such prestige that he was not obliged to remove his headdress in the presence of the doge.

after the fire of 1577, Antonio a Ponte (c 1512-97) was given a mere 16 months to complete the Palace's reconstruction.

The prison cells located in the Palace, meanwhile, were referred to as the **Pozzi e Piombi** (**Wells and Leads**): the *Pozzi* were the sinister, deep and damp dungeons for hardened criminals; the *Piombi*, so-called because they were roofed in lead, for prisoners "doing time" for a couple of months. Life in the cells was not necessarily that severe: prisoners were allowed to bring some furniture and a little money with them; lawyers were allowed to continue to perform certain professional duties. Punishment was intended to induce remorse by exerted psychological pressure rather than by inflicting physical suffering and harsh living conditions. It was from the *Piombi* that **Giacomo Casanova** (1725-98) made his daring escape, emerging onto the roof above the Grand Council Chamber.

■ Ponte dei Sospiri★★

The world-famous Bridge of Sighs owes its name to Romantic literary notions: overwhelmed by the enchanting view from the windows of this bridge, this was where the prisoners would suffer their final torment.

The bridge, constructed in Istrian stone, links the palace with the Prigioni Nuove (New Prisons). It was built during the dogeship of **Marino Grimani** (1595-1605) and bears his coat of arms. Inside, the bridge is divided into two passages through which visitors pass on their tour of the Doges' Palace. Given the number of rooms and the length of the tour, it is easy to lose one's bearings and to cross the bridge without realising it – so beware! ■

When ships were built in a day and napkins were made of sugar...

Da Ponte was obliged to draw upon the formidable skills of the *arsenalotti* who, as demonstrated to Henry III on his visit to Venice in 1574, were capable of assembling a ship in one day. This same day, pastrymakers made the banquet into a sumptuous occasion in honour of the sovereign. The table featured spectacular mythological and historical sculptures contrived by their skilled artistry: Henry III attempted to open out his napkin, which was fashioned out of sugar, so realistic it appeared, before realising that it was a subtle joke.

ON THE SQUARE

■ Torre dell'Orologio

Designed by Codussi (c 1440-1504), the clock tower was erected between 1496 and 1499, and is the main entrance to the Mercerie.

The astronomical quadrant probably attracts less attention than the two Moors who sound the hour on a big bell at the top of the tower.

Below it, the lion passant of St Mark is set against a starry background. Below this tier comes a Virgin and Child before whom, on Ascension Day, appear mechanical figurines of the Three Kings. The Roman numerals *(left)* tell the hour and the minutes are marked out at intervals of five to the right.

■ Museo Correr★★

Next to the Ara Napoleonica which bounds the square to the west, the museum traces the 1 000 year-old history of the city: paintings, sculpture and artefacts.

It takes its name from **Teodor Correr** (1750-1830), a Venetia gentleman who wanted to leav his rich collection of artefacts re lating to the history and art of th Serenissima to the city. It house sculptures by **Antonio Canov** (1757-1822), doges' *corni* (caps staffs of command, and *manin* (modelled hands used, along wit the ballot urn, for counting vote in the lengthy procedure in elec ing a doge).

The **Collezione Numismatic** (Numismatic Collection) com prises almost the entire series o coinage minted by the Republi including the famous **zecchino** the suggestive *Pietà★*, marked b brittle form and metallic colour, the work of **Cosmè Tura** (c 1430 1495). His attention to detail, us

One of the Mo bellstrikers in a

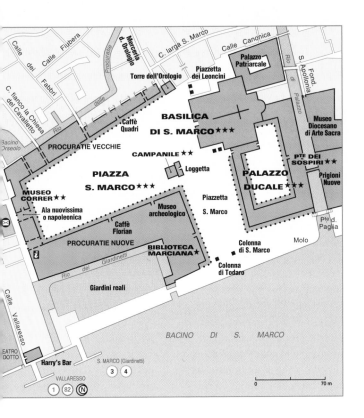

f colour and sensitive modelling f the face of the Madonna may be nfluenced by Flemish painting.

room is dedicated to **Bar-olomeo Vivarini** (c 1432-91), who came from Murano. His works betray the strong influence f Mantegna (1431-1506).

he only work by Antonello da Messina (c 1430-79), who visited Venice in 1475/6 is a *Pietà***. Unfortunately, the ochre ground of the faces have permeated the delicate glazes, damage aggravated y earlier attempts at restoration.

The landscape vignette of the Church of St Francis in Messina, however, is easily discernible.

The Bellinis are gathered together in one room (*Pietà** by **Giovanni** - 1430-1516).

There are works by **Vittore Carpaccio** (c 1460-1526); his *Two Venetian Ladies* have slightly dismissive expressions. According to some, the panel with the two courtesans is a fragment of a diptych, its companion piece (a valley hunting scene) being in the JP Getty Museum in Malibu. The

pictures depict two bored ladies of noble birth, attested by the coat of arms on the vase, awaiting the return of their husbands or lovers from a hunting expedition.

The *Gentleman in the Red Cap*★★ (1490-1495) is attributed to a painter from Ferrara/Bologna, although in the past it was thought to have been executed by Lotto

(c 1480-1556), Giovanni Bellini o Carpaccio. It is somewhat irksom and disconcerting not to be able t meet the man's noble and inqui ing look, as he turns his back o a landscape that is lapped by th water of a lake or a river.

One room is dedicated to th **Bucintoro**, the doge's ship aboar which the Marriage with the Se

The Marriage with the Sea

According to one version, a fisherman obtained the ring from St Mark on the night that Satan threatened to destroy Venice with a storm.

Another legend relates that on Ascension Day, the doge solemnly proclaimed from the *Bucintoro* (state barge), in Latin *"We wed you, o sea, as a sign of true and perpetual dominion»*, casting a gold ring into the sea as he spoke.

The ceremony began outside St Mark's, where the procession rallied before continuing on to the fort of San Andrea near the Lido. There the ring was cast into the sea. On his return, the doge stopped at San Nicolò on the Lido to attend Mass.

ook place. The ship was 35m/115ft ong and 7m/23ft wide. Propelled by 68 rowers, it could only sail in the almost meteorological conditions, ecause, being as tall as it was, it ould easily have tipped over.

Of particular interest are the vid, typically Venetian topo-raphical works of the German rtist Joseph Heintz the Younger 1600-78), including *Bull Baiting* Campo San Polo.

Other exhibits include a collec-on of "end products": textiles ade by the weavers' guild, shoes roduced by the *calegheri* (cob-ers) guild.

he *Giochi* (Games) collection in-ludes examples of the Strength of lercules or human pyramids that ere "built" on wooden platforms n the Thursday before Lent and ther feast days; fist fights (*Guerre ei Pugni*) that developed between he rival Castellani, who were mostly sailors, and Nicolotti, who were mostly fishermen; and bull-baiting (*Caccia ai Tori*), during which dogs that had been excited to a frenzy would be unleashed.

■ Libreria Sansoviniana★

This noble and harmonious build-ing was designed by Sansovino in 1553. At No 7 is a library, **Biblio-teca Nazionale Marciana**, where it is possible to view manuscripts, maps and engravings.

■ Museo Archeologico

The Archaeological Museum is housed in the Procuratie Nuove, two doors away from the Bib-lioteca Marciana. It houses Greek sculpture, Egyptian and Roman fragments and a collection of coins and medals. ■

THE MOST BEAUTIFUL BEAUTIFUL STREET IN VENICE

IL CANAL GRANDE★★★

When he was living in Palazzo Mocenigo, Lord Byron used to swim across the Grand Canal. Mark Twain described its appearance in moonlight as magical; Goethe felt himself to be "Lord of the Adriatic" here; and Dickens, convinced the ghost of Shylock roamed the bridges of the city, felt the spirit of Shakespeare strongly in Venice. To best experience the Grand Canal, take a vaporetto from the railway station, described by Gustav von Aschenbach, the main character in *Death in Venice*, as the "tradesmen's entrance" to the city, and follow it round to Piazza San Marco, the heart of the city. This short journey will undoubtedly leave as magical an impression on modern-day travellers as it once did on its illustrious visitors of the past.

Given the nature and origins of Venice as it seemingly rises up out of the water (although actually built on islands), the Grand Canal is, in every respect, the city's high street.

The Grand Canal (3km/2mi long, between 30m/98ft and 70m/229ft wide and, on average, 5.5m/18ft deep) takes the form of an inverted S, with the bend marked by the Ca' Foscari. It is not the only way through the city and it is often quicker to go on foot but, with the best views of the *palazzi* and churches that overlook the canal, it is an experience not to be missed.

From river to canal

The origins of the Grand Canal, which may once have been a branch of the River Medoacus are lost in the mists of time. The *traghetti* (gondolas which cross the river) have, however, provided a ferry service between the banks of the canal since the year 1000: some of the existing landing stages have been in situ since the 13C, many either serving mills that were operated by the tides or *squeri* where the gondolas were built; then there were the workshops or the Guild of Wool Weavers and Clothmakers.

The finest walk takes one along the canal where the beauty of the city unfolds: façades of vibrant colours, resplendent with gilding, exude the festive spirit and optimism of the Venetians, who have never known the threat of oppression, not even in the Middle Ages, when the rest of the world had to build fortresses and sombre palaces to defend themselves. The *palazzi* that flank the Grand Canal are the Venetian nobility's expression of pride and self-satisfaction: they were the only people who could vouchsafe a piece of this water garden.

Although commercial, banking and state enterprises have been in operation along the canal since the Renaissance, churches and fine *palazzi* were being erected right up until the Republic breathed its last. ∎

The Canal Grande between Salute and Accademia

■ Stazione di Santa Lucia

It has marked the entrance to the city since 1860 when the first station was built. The present building was erected in 1954.

■ Gli Scalzi

This Baroque church was designed by Longhena (1598-1682). Its most distinctive features are the niches in the façade (1672-78), which are adorned with statues and framed with paired columns.

■ Ponte degli Scalzi

The original construction (1858) was undertaken by the civil engineer, Neville, who was also responsible for the first Accademia Bridge. It was rebuilt in 1934.

■ San Geremia

From the water all that can be seen of the Church of St Jerome is the Chapel of Saint Lucy, which houses the remains of the Sicilian martyr.

■ Palazzo Labia★★

This elegant 18C residence on the corner of the Cannaregio Canal is slightly set back from the Grand Canal. The ground floor is rusticated, with Ionic and Corinthian pilasters on the two floors above; the large windows open out onto balconies. The eagles which protrude from under the roof refer to the heraldry of the Labia family.

■ San Marcuola

This church is distinctive from others overlooking the Grand Canal: the roughly-bricked façade remains incomplete. Interestingly, this is actually the side of the church. Its present appearance is Baroque in style, but the church is much older.

Fish, boats, sea horses: even the capitals in Rialto are inspired by the sea

The ostentations of the Labia family

Perhaps a little maliciously, legend has it that at the end of a banquet the Labia family would hurl their gold dinner plates and cutlery out of the window and into the canal to cries proclaiming their indifference to their wealth. The infamous family was more astute, however, than they might have appeared, for by placing fishing nets at the bottom of the canal, they were later able to retrieve their precious treasure for use another day.

■ Palazzo Vendramin Calergi★

This Renaissance palace was commissioned by the noble family of Loredan al Codussi, who worked in the city between 1502 and 1504. With composite three-arched windows, it is a synthesis of Byzantine and Gothic architectural features. Here, **Richard Wagner** lived and worked. The *palazzo* currently serves as the winter headquarters of the municipal casino (plans are afoot to use it for a different purpose).

■ Ca' d'Oro★★★

Much restoration work has recaptured the *palazzo's* former glory: its façade, a subtle creation in the ornate Gothic style, presents a colonnade lapped by the water's edge – proof of its use as a warehouse as well as a residence – and, on the upper floors, two enclosed loggias with arched windows, interlaced with intersecting tracery and quatrefoils. Curiously, this decorative feature is not centred in the façade. The right section consists of a blank wall between single-arched windows. The corners are accentuated by cordons of marble. The *palazzo* houses the

Galleria Franchetti which contains the famous painting of *Saint Sebastian*** by **Andrea Mantegna** (1431-1506).

■ Ca' da Mosto

Erected in the 13C, this Veneto-Byzantine *palazzo* was where Alvise da Mosto (1432-88) was born, the great navigator who explored the western coast of Africa as far as Cape Verde. The portico betrays the building's dual function as house and warehouse. Note the first-floor ceiling decorated with circular coffering or patera. Between the 16C and 18C, the *palazzo* served as the city's finest hotel, the Leon Bianco.

■ Fondaco dei Tedeschi

This 13C *palazzo* served as the headquarters of German traders and as a warehouse for their goods. Devastated by fire (1505-08), it was rebuilt by Giorgio Spavento (in Venice between the 15C and 16C) and by Scarpagnino (in Venice between 1505 and 1549). The façade that overlooks the Grand Canal, at one time frescoed by Giorgione (c 1476-1510) and Titian (1490-1576), has a portico on the ground floor, as befitted a *fondaco* (warehouse). It houses the main post office.

■ Ponte di Rialto**

The **Rialto Bridge** is the most important crossing point between the two banks of the Grand Canal. Although today's bridge is the sixth version – the original was built in 1175 – this is the first stone-built construction. The work of Antonio da Ponte was opened in 1591. The shops, housed in the symmetrical arcades, were originally used by bankers and moneylenders, in proximity to the first Zecca.

Palazzo Loredan

Also a *fondaco* (warehouse), this Veneto-Byzantine *palazzo* retains original features: part of the portico and windows opening out onto the loggia, interlaced with pateras, run the length of the first floor. Palazzo Loredan and the nearby Palazzo Farsetti now accommodate municipal offices.

Palazzo Lando Corner Spinelli

This Renaissance *palazzo* erected in 1490 was probably designed by Mauro Codussi. The façade in Istrian stone is heavily rusticated. The upper storeys are punctuated with typical two-light windows, and a Renaissance frieze of festoons runs below the attic windows.

Palazzo Mocenigo

This building comprises four adjacent *palazzi*. The first dates back to 1579, when it was rebuilt according to the designs of Alessandro Vittoria. The second and third buildings, which are identical, are from the end of the 16C; the last, the so-called "Casa Vecchia", a Gothic construction, was remodelled by Francesco Contin during the first half of the 17C. Previous inhabitants of this group of *palazzi* include Giordano Bruno (1548-1600) and **Lord Byron** (1788-1824), who started work on his *Don Juan* here. The English "Don Giovanni" often swam home from a day at San Lazzaro or an evening at the Lido: a habit that instituted a swimming race that was held until 1949 and rewarded by the Byron Cup.

Palazzo Grassi★

Erected in 1749 by Giorgio Massari (1687-1766), possibly Venice's greatest architect in the first half of the 18C, this last Venetian palace to be built before the fall of the Republic is designed with all the majesty of neo-Classical domestic architecture at its best. Inside, the courtyard has a fine colonnade and a grand staircase frescoed by Alessandro Longhi (1733-1813) populated with masked figures. Other rooms are frescoed by Jacopo Guarana (1720-1808) and Fabio Canal (1703-67). Today the building is used for prestigious temporary exhibitions.

Ponte dell'Accademia

Venice had to wait until 1854 for its second and third means of crossing the Grand Canal after the Rialto Bridge. The original iron construction, restricted in height, hindered the passage of the *vaporettos*; the bridge was replaced in 1932, and built of wood because of lack of funds. The present bridge is a copy of it.

■ Palazzo Cavalli Franchetti

The splendid façade of this late-15C *palazzo*, complete with delicate tracery work, five-arched windows with intersecting tracery and quatrefoil motifs, casts its intricate reflection across the Grand Canal. It was rebuilt towards the end of the 19C by Camillo Boito, the brother of the musician.

■ Palazzo Corner della Ca' Granda

Nowadays this Renaissance palac is used as the police headquar ters *(Prefettura)*. It was built fo the nephew of Caterina Cornar by Sansovino (1486-1570). Th rusticated ground floor has three-arch portico; elegantl aligned arched windows on th upper floors alternate with paire columns. ■

View of the left bank from Ponte dell'Accademia. On the left, Palazzo Cavalli Franchetti

N. Bosques-MICHELIN

RIGHT BANK

■ San Simeon Piccolo

This is the first eye-catching landmark on leaving the station. Its distinctive features include a Corinthian pronaos (front portico) up a flight of steps and a green dome. The church was designed by Scalfarotto (c 1700-64) in the tradition set by Palladio (1508-80) and Longhena (1598-1682).

■ Ponte degli Scalzi

Originally built in 1858, the bridge was designed by the same civil engineer, Neville, as the first Accademia Bridge. It was rebuilt in 1934.

■ Fondaco dei Turchi

This 13 C Veneto-Byzantine *fondaco* was heavily restored in the 19C. It was built as a private house and turned into commercial premises in 1621. With the side towers framing the façade, the portico and the floor above are laced with arches. Between 1621 and 1838 the warehouse was used by Turks, hence its name. Nowadays the building houses the Natural History Museum.

■ Fondaco del Megio

This very distinctive building with its walls of roughly hewn brick and tiny windows dates back to the 15C. Note the lion that stands out below the ornate crenellation. The Fondaco del Megio was used as a general grain store, notably for millet (*miglio = megio* – hence the name).

■ San Stae

Dedicated to St Eustace, this church was renovated during the 17C. The elaborate Baroque façade (1709), dominated by a pedimented bay set between two roughcast wings, is attributed to Domenico Rossi (1678-1742). Its broken tympanum, crowned with statues over the entrance, is original. Inside a single nave are works by Piazzetta (1683-1754), Ricci (1659-1734) and Tiepolo (1696-1770). Doge Alvise Mocenigo is buried here.

■ Ca' Pesaro★

At the death of Baldassare Longhena (1598-1682), completion of the building was assigned to Antonio Gaspari (c 1670-c 1730). Unusual is its diamond-pointed rustication of the ground floor and row of lions' heads. Great arched windows with single columns give onto an open loggia (*2nd and 3rd floors*). It now houses the **Museum of Oriental Art** and the **International Gallery of Modern Art**.

Ca' Corner della Regina

Designed by Domenico Rossi (1678-1742), the heavily rusticated ground floor gives way to plainer upper storeys punctuated by balconies and windows framed with columns. It houses the National Archives of Contemporary Art.

Pescheria

The portico of this neo-Gothic building, which dates back to the beginning of the 20C, now accommodates the fish market, hence the name.

Fabbriche Nuove

This rather plain building on the bend of the Grand Canal, was designed by **Sansovino** (1486-1570). The ground floor at one time consisted of *magazzini* (small shops) and warehousing. The first floor was occupied by magistrates' courts ruling on commercial matters.

Fabbriche Vecchie

Destroyed by fire, the warehouse were rebuilt by Scarpagnino (activ in Venice between 1505 and 1549 The "old workshops" boast the own columned portico.

Palazzo dei Camerlenghi

This Renaissance palace situated i the lee of the bridge was designe by Guglielmo dei Grigi, or "Berga masco" (active in Venice betwee c 1515-30), for the Camerlengh (government officials responsible for the State's financial affairs). Th pentagonal building has large win dows below a frieze of festoons.

Daily business in the Rialto market

N. Bosques-MICHELIN

■ Ponte di Rialto★★

The **Rialto Bridge** is the most important crossing point between the two banks of the Grand Canal. Although today's bridge is the sixth version – the original was built in 1175 – this is the first stone-built construction. The work of Antonio da Ponte, it was opened in 1591. The shops which are housed in the symmetrical arcades were originally used by money changers, bankers and moneylenders.

■ Palazzo Bernardo

Gothic in style (1442), the building boasts splendid five-arched windows, pointed on the first floor, and quatrefoils on the second floor.

■ Palazzo Pisani Moretta

Also late Gothic, the Palazzo dates from the second half of the 15C. The windows have intersecting tracery that enclose quatrefoils on the upper floors.

■ Palazzo Balbi

The façade of this *palazzo*, attributed to Alessandro Vittoria (1525-c 1600), is divided into three sections. Above a rusticated ground floor, the central bay is pierced by an arrangement of three arched windows. Note the two distinctive large coats of arms and the obelisks on the roof.

■ Ca' Foscari

The glorious façade of this *palazzo* rises above the Grand Canal at the junction with the Rio Foscari. Perfect symmetry aligns the three orders of arched windows, arranged in groups that alternate with simple, single light openings and stonework. The original 14C building was rebuilt closer to the water's edge after 1550, resulting in an overall Gothic design with early Renaissance features (marble low relief above the ornate arcade of windows on the second floor). Nowadays it forms part of the university.

■ Ca' Rezzonico★★

This house was to be the last palace to be designed by Baldassare Longhena (1598-1682), before Giorgio Massari (c 1686-1766) took over. It houses the **Museum of 18C Venice** which contains collections of Venetian finery and works by Tiepolo, Canaletto, Longhi and Guardi.

Engaged columns punctuate the bays of the rusticated ground level as well as the arched openings on the first and attic storeys. Note the extensive embellishment of the *piano nobile* and the fine configuration of balconies.

■ Palazzo Moro

Situated just beyond the Ca' Rezzonico vaporetto stop, beyond the gracious Palazzo Stern and its gardens overlooking the Grand Canal, this 16C *palazzo* is austere in its simplicity. It was here that the Moro family resided, one of whom suffered the tragic marriage that was to inspire **Shakespeare** (1564-1616) to write *Othello*, and portray the famous "Moor of Venice" as black.

■ Palazzo Loredan dell'Ambasciatore

The late-Gothic Palazzo Loredan has splendid arched windows with a quatrefoil design. Between the single-arched windows at the sides are two shield-bearing pages.

■ Accademia★★★

The Academy of Fine Arts has been housed here since the beginning of the 19C. Whereas the former Scuola Grande della Carità is Gothic in style, its 18C façade is by Giorgio Massari and Bernardo Maccurzzi. The church, rebuilt between 1441 and 1452, most probably under the guidance of Bartolomeo Bon, has been subject to restoration through the ages: it involved Palladio (1508-80).

■ Ponte dell'Accademia

Venice had to wait until 1854 for its two additional means of crossing the Grand Canal after

The delicate tracery work of the windows of a palace on the Grand Canal

he Rialto Bridge. The original iron construction, restricted in height, hindered the passage of the vaporettos; the bridge was therefore replaced in 1932, this time built of wood because of lack of funds. The present bridge is a copy of it.

Palazzo Barbarigo

The mosaics which decorate the façade depict Charles V in Titian's studio and Henry III of France on Murano. These were installed by the glass-blowers and mosaic-makers, the Compagnia Venezia e Murano, responsible for the reconstruction of the 16C palace towards the end of the 19C.

Palazzo Venier dei Leoni

It requires a great deal of imagination to conjure up a picture of how the palace was intended to look by its designer Lorenzo Boschetti in 1749, despite the scale model of the building in the Correr Museum. The Venier family were forced to stop work on the building because of financial problems; all that survives of the original is its rusticated ground floor.

The allusion to lions might stem from a story that the Venier family managed to tame a lion in the garden, or otherwise, more simply, to the lion masks along the base. The building currently houses the **Peggy Guggenheim Collection**.

■ Ca' Dario★

This small, late-15C *palazzo* is most distinctively embellished with polychrome marble decoration. It was built by the Lombardo family for Giovanni Dario, the Secretary to the Senate of the Republic at the Sultan's court. It has gained a sinister reputation as a result of mysterious circumstances surrounding the death of several of the building's owners.

■ Palazzo Salviati

Like Palazzo Barbarigo, the 19C Palazzo Salviati was owned by glass-makers who provided its fine mosaics.

■ Santa Maria della Salute★★

The massive white structure with its distinctive spiral volutes (the *orecchioni* = big ears) is visible from afar. Designed by Longhena (1598-1682), it was erected upon the wishes of the doge as a supplication to end the plague of 1630: a story recounted in *I Promessi Sposi* by Alessandro Manzoni.

■ Dogana da Mar

It was here on this extension of the Dorsoduro that goods used to be unloaded and duty on them levied. The present construction – dominated by a tower on which two atlantes support the weight of the World and the figure of Fortune – dates back to the second half of the 17C. ■

Museums, Scuole and surroundings

GALLERIE DELL'ACCADEMIA★★★

The **Academy of Fine Art** exhibits an important collection of art works encapsulating the development of Venetian painting from the 14C to the 18C.

Sala I – The room is devoted to Venetian Gothic masters from the 14C and the first half of the 15C.

Sala II – This room displays important 15C altarpieces: the *Crucifixion and Apotheosis of the Ten Thousand Martyrs of Mount Ararat* by **Vittore Carpaccio** (c 1465-c 1526) depicts the legendary massacre of the Roman soldiers betrayed by their own captains after beating the Armenian rebels; the famous *Virgin and Child with Saints*, also known as the *Pala di San Giobbe*, by Giovanni Bellini (c 1470-1516); the *Agony in the Garden* by Marco Basaiti (c 1470-c 1530) and the *Presentation of Christ in the Temple* by Vittorio Carpaccio *(left)*.

The *Calling of the Sons of Zebedee*, by Marco Basaiti, is a particularly beautiful and engaging treatment of the subject of Christ recruiting his Apostles, the variety of scenery with the focus on the water and the magical quality of the colour *(centre)*.

Sala IV – *St George* by **Andrea Mantegna** (1431-1506) hangs on the wall to the left. The painting has a Tuscan feel about it. To the right, Giovanni Bellini's *Madonna*

A reflection on the altarpiece of San Giobbe

This altarpiece bears the name of one of the Patriarchs (the figure closest to the Madonna, *right*), to whom the church is dedicated: the pilasters are matched exactly to the position they were intended to occupy above the second altar *(right)*.

Bellini was influenced by the San Cassiano altarpiece by Antonello da Messina, although he embues his figures with a more solemn dignity, culminating in the most important of the group, the Madonna, and the bright light refracted across the mosaic floor.

with Child between St Catherine and Mary Magdalene depicts four figures thrown into relief by a strong transverse light that lifts them out of the darkness. In contrast is the *Portrait of a Young Man* by the Dutch artist Hans Memling (c 1435-94) with its sharp delineation of features and characterisation; lost in tranquil meditation, the young man's face is embued with inner calm.

Sala V – *The Tempest* by **Giorgione** (c 1467-1510) is the crystallisation of a state of mind rather than the representation of a specific moment in time. The protagonists are the three figures, the ruins, the water and the village caught in an iridescent green light by a flash of lightning. Another famous work by Giorgione, *The Old Woman,* is a compelling portrait, touched with the inevitable sadness of realised awareness, highlighted by the inscription in the cartouche *col tempo* – with time. The *Allegories* by Giovanni Bellini are particularly exquisite small paintings intended as decorative panels to set into a piece of furniture or mirror. By the same artist are the *Madonna and the Seraphim* and the *Madonna under the Trees.* The title refers to the trees which serve as foreground to the landscape, channelling perspective across the countryside to distant snow-capped peaks.

Sala VII – This little room is home to the famous *Portait of a Young*

Gentleman in his Study by **Lorenzo Lotto** (c 1480-1577); the sitter's concentration seems to have been interrupted by a thought or a memory; distracted from his reading, his long delicate fingers idly flick through the pages as he muses perhaps upon the passing of time, staring into the distance, his pale, chiselled face contrasting with his black coat.

Sala X – The *Pietà* by **Titian** (1490-1576) was intended by the artist for his own tomb at the Frari but remained unfinished on his death. Note on the right, at the Sibyl's feet, the hand raised in supplication.

Opposite the entrance hang **Tintoretto's canvases** depicting the life of St Mark: the *Theft of the Body of St Mark*, the *Finding of the Body of St Mark* (which is now in the Brera Collection in Milan). Note how the figures in the foreground appear thrown into relief by the use of chiaroscuro, where forms, picked out by strong light, are contrasted against another recessed into shadow; here phantom-like figures fade into the darkness, sloping off in search of safety in the palace.

The whole of the right wall is taken by **Veronese's** controversial *Christ in the House of Levi,* conceived as a *Last Supper.* However, Veronese was summoned before a tribunal of the Inquisition on a charge of heresy. He promptly changed the painting's title.

A Flemish Italian?

Vittore Carpaccio (1455-1526), following in the wake of Bellini and Antonello, suffuses the lessons learnt from Flemish painting with his own personal creativity. Carpaccio surpassed Bellini in sensitivity and in his inimitable talent for story-telling. His pictures are imaginatively populated with well-observed and delightful details: he even manages to reconcile his penchant for miniaturist precision with a love of broad views. Landscapes are a key element in his paintings, representing luxuriant, flowery vegetation, inhabited by a host of animals. Renaissance buildings stand out, embellished with marble inlays that might have been designed by the Lombardo family and surrounded by numerous oriental motifs such as palm trees and Moorish turbans. All of Carpaccio's works display the same distinctive features: boldness of line, luminosity, vivid colours, perfect sense of proportion, attention to detail and a love of crowd scenes.

Sala XI – Her are works by **Giambattista Tiepolo** (1696-1770) and the masterpiece by Bonifacio de' Pitati (c 1487-1553): the *Rich Man Epulone* projects a tranquil scene, rich with incidental detail and contrasting personality, populated with musicians, a beggar, huntsmen and lovers converging in a wood, as a fire rages on the right.

The next rooms are full of the most typical Venetian paintings by **Canaletto** (1697-1768), Bernardo Bellotto (1721-80); **Francesco Guardi** (1712-93); Giambattista Piazzetta (1683-1754); Rosalba Carriera (1675-1758) and Pietro Longhi (1702-85). Room XVI accommodates works from the 18C, including the *Fortune-teller* by Piazzetta.(Sala XVIa).

Sala XX – It contains the famous collection of paintings illustrating the story of the *Miracles of the Relic of the True Cross*, executed between the 15C and 16C.

The *Procession in St Mark's Square* by **Gentile Bellini** (1429-1507) covers the wall facing the entrance. The work is an important representation of the square in the mid-15C.

Carpaccio's *Miracle of the Relic of the True Cross at Rialto* can be seen on the entrance wall. Interestingly, the subject of the painting – the miraculous healing of a madman taking place on the first-floor loggia on the left – seems secondary to the prousion of topographical detail showing Venice at the end of the 15C: the wooden Rialto Bridge.

Sala XXI – This room contains the colourful and magical series of canvases by **Carpaccio** that retell the **Story of St Ursula**.

The first panel, *Arrival of the English Ambassadors,* shows the ambassadors arriving at the (Catholic) court in Brittany bearing a proposal of marriage from their English (pagan) prince, Hereus. Ursula *(to the right)* is shown dictating her conditions of marriage in the presence of her wet nurse seated on the steps.

The next scene shows *The English Ambassadors Taking their Leave*, in which the king hands over the reply: it may well be that it is being written up by the scribe who is concentrating on his task.

In the *Return of the Ambassadors* the cortège bringing the reply to the king is followed by a crowd to the edge of the lagoon. The central scene is almost theatrical, the eye caught by the handsome youth turning away as if affronted; the figure sitting on the bank is the "Steward", whose duty it is to herald the arrival of the ambassadors, invited by the doge, with music, while a monkey on the right watches a guinea fowl.

The *Meeting of Ursula and Hereus and the Departure of the Pilgrims* is a composite scene, divided by the pennant, showing the prince taking his leave; Hereus and Ursula bid farewell to the rulers of Brittany before departing for Rome. Note the sharp contrast between the harsh, darkened representation of the English capital on the left and the colourful Breton town on the right, represented according to Humanist ideals.

In Ursula's Dream the scene is more compact, set in Ursula's room where the light reveals more domestic details: reminiscent of St Augustine in his Studio, the angel reaches out for the palm of martyrdom.

The Meeting of the Pilgrims with Pope Cyriac under the Walls of Rome takes place against the background of the Castel Sant'Angelo, between two groups of virgin pilgrims (Ursula's companions) to the left and the prelates to the right. In the centre, the betrothed are waiting to be crowned.

The *Arrival in Cologne* depicts how, on their arrival in the city, Ursula and her father, who has joined the pilgrims, learn that the city is in the hands of the Huns.

Ursula's eventful life on earth concludes with the *Martyrdom of the Pilgrims and Ursula's Funeral*, in which the two scenes are separated by the column. In the centre the warrior is removing blood from his sword.

The final panel in the cycle, however, showing the *Apotheosis of St Ursula and her Companions*, is perhaps the saddest. ■

■ San Trovaso

This church is dedicated to two saints (Gervasius and Protasius) whose names have been contracted to "Trovaso". The original church was built in the 9C, but underwent much subsequent reconstruction, culminating in its total remodelling by architects of the Palladian School between the 16C and 17C. It boasts two lateral façades with two huge windows in an arched semicircle, a relatively common feature in Venice.

It contains works by Tintoretto's son Domenico (c 1560-1635), Michele Giambono (active 1420-62), Domenico Tintoretto and Palma il Giovane (1548-1628). The organ (1765) was made by Gaetano Callido.

Further along the Rio di San Trovaso between the church and the Zattere is a quaint boatyard. To reach the Church of the Gesuati proceed along the Zattere in the direction of the Dogana.

■ Gesuati

The Church of Santa Maria del Rosario ai Gesuati is dedicated to the Madonna of the Rosary, honoured by a 14C order of laymen. The incumbent order of Domini-cans commissioned the architect Giorgio Massari (c 1686-1766) to remodel the building.

The luminous interior comprises one nave lined with three chapels on either side. The sculptural decoration is almost entirely attributable to Giovanni Maria Morlaiter (1699-1781). Typically 18C in style, the church has only one element which does not belong to this century, even if it was restored in the 18C by Piazzetta: the *Crucifixion* by Tintoretto (1518-94) above the third altar on the left.

Continue towards the railway station, as far as S. Barnabas square. From here, *calle Lunga* leads to San Sebastiano.

■ San Sebastiano★★

The white façade of the church betrays the complexity of the internal structure: columns in the lower section outline the form of the side chapels, those in the upper part echo the choir stalls.

The "entrance" area is defined by the monks' choir stalls, which extend across the aisles and side chapels.

Note the opulent quality of **Veronese's** art; it was with this cycle of frescoes that the painter (1528-

Squero di San Trovaso

588) was particularly preoccu-
pied for the most significant part
of his life. His friend and colleague,
a monk with whom he shared the
commission, left Veronese complete freedom of composition and
expression. Veronese started with
a *Coronation of the Virgin* on the ceiling in the sacristy, to include *Four
Evangelists (side panels)*. Colour
– notably red and blue – is used
to associate the figure of Mary
with the Christ-child; God the
Father is robed in greeny blue. **St
Sebastian** recurs as the subject of
many of the frescoes in this church.
In a depiction of *St Sebastian before
Diocletian,* the saint wounded by an
arrow is watched by two people
on the balcony as he reproaches
the persecutor of the Christians.
Opposite, the *Martyrdom of St
Sebastian* seems to be theatrically
enacted between four columns.
Head towards the church of Angelo Raffaele. Cross the river, then
turn left.

■ San Nicolò dei Mendicoli

The dedication of the church to
the *Mendicoli* alludes to the beggars
and down at heel who used to live
in the area, notably the *pinzochere*
(impoverished religious women)
who sheltered in the portico.
The indications are that the church
was founded in the 7C, although
this building dates for the most
part from the 12C, as does the
massive bell-tower.
Come back along the Fondamenta
and cross the canal by the *Campo
dei Carmine*.

■ Scuola Grande dei Carmini★

The narrowest end of the great
Campo di Santa Margherita becomes the *Scuola dei Carmini* (Guild
of Dyers), beyond which is the
square of the same name, dominated by the façade of their church.
The two façades of the Scuola have
been widely attributed to Longhena (1598-1682). The *Scuola* contains works by **Giovanni Battista
Tiepolo** (1696-1770). ■

MUSEO STORICO NAVALE

The museum comprises four floors and houses a large collection of artefacts: a torpedo, taffrail lights, mortars, cannons, scale models of the city and her fortresses, firearms and sabres.

On the first floor are examples of wooden sculptures which decorated the galleys, coats of arms, naval weaponry, nautical instruments, parchments (pilots' charts and navigation material specifying details of coastal areas, harbours...), engravings, models of ships, fine examples of galleys' broadsides, the supposed remains of Lazzarro Mocenigo's flagship which disappeared in the Dardanelles in 1657 and a model of the state barge, the *Bucintoro*.

The second floor is dedicated to naval history during the 19C and 20C and includes scale models and naval uniforms.

The third floor displays an extensive collection of ex-votos, luxury vessel from the 18C, gondolas and a model of the Squero di San Trovaso.

On the fourth floor is a section dedicated to the Swedish navy and its relationship with Venice. The rescue expedition involving the airship *Italia* is remembered here.

On leaving the main building, follow the Rio dell'Arsenale to the second section of the museum on the right.

Even though the vessels are not displayed in their full glory in this setting, the pavilions house some interesting craft: a 1932 hydrofoil used for racing, a torpedo-launch (1942), an 1890 diving vessel and the remains of the steam ship *Elettra*.

Venice out to watch the historic regatta

The Arsenal*

In addition to being the naval base, a depository for arms and equipment and a workshop where maintenance work was carried out, the Arsenal also served as the main shipyard – popularly thought of as the very heart of the Venetian State. The toponymy serves as a reminder of the various trades and activities of each street: Calle della Pegola (fish), Calle dei Bombardieri (cannon-ball foundries), Calle del Piombo (lead), and Calle delle Ancore (anchors). Mills continuously churned out hemp rope; other structures included the sail lofts, the artillery warehouses and the slipways.

The first recorded dockyard in Venice, the **Arsenale Vecchio**, dates back to about 1104 when the demands of the crusades stimulated shipbuilding activity. The chosen zone, between the towers and the Galeazzi Canal, was protected and linked to the Bacino di San Marco by a canal that was only wide enough to accommodate one boat at a time. At one time, there were 24 active boatyards. Along the slipways, the hulls were aligned in two rows.

In the 14C, the Arsenal was extended towards the southeast (**Arsenale Nuovo**). Altogether 16 000 *marangoni* were employed, men apprenticed as joiners and trained as shipwrights. The boat-building techniques were highly advanced for their time, as the Venetians were already implementing production lines.

During the second half of the 15C, the **Arsenale Nuovissimo** was extended to the north of the area – on the Galeazzi Canal (1564).

Having been destroyed during the French occupation (1797), the Arsenal was then rebuilt by the Austrians between 1814 and 1830. After the Venetians attacked it in 1848 the area was abandoned during the third Austrian occupation (1849-66). Restructuring work was initiated during the second half of the 19C, and continued to 1914.

Enclosed within medieval walls punctuated with towers, the Arsenal has two main entrances along the Rio dell'Arsenale: one for land-based craft and one for the water-borne.

The land entrance, a grand Renaissance triumphal arch, constitutes the most important gateway, dating back to c 1460, presided over by the lions from Ancient Greece (Athens and Piraeus), brought over by Francesco Morosini after his victory over Morea in 1687.

The water entrance through which the vaporetto passes, is marked by two towers which were rebuilt in 1686.

AROUND THE
MUSEO NAVALE

Further along the Fondamenta di Fronte is the bridge which leads into the Campo dell'Arsenale, under the watchful eyes of the famous lions. Here the visitor enters an almost traffic-free zone of quiet alleyways and peaceful squares. A short walk will eventually lead to the Church of San Francesco della Vigna.

Proceed along the Fondamenta di Fronte into Campo San Martino. Cross the bridge at the Fondamenta Penini and turn left into Calle delle Muneghette. In Campiello Due Pozzi, take Calle del Mandolin on the left. Turn right into Calle degli Scudi which leads directly to Campo di San Francesco della Vigna.

Coming from the south is particularly interesting as the route passes between the columns of an unusual 19C portico, of a delicate pinkish-brown colour, which links the naval headquarters with the Renaissance Palazzo Gritti, otherwise known as *La Nunziatura* (the Nunciature). Originally owned by **Doge Andrea Gritti** (1523-38), it was ceded by the Republic to Pope Pius IV (1559-65), who allowed it to be used by Apostolic delegates.

■ San Francesco della Vigna★

There really were vineyards here when the Franciscans first erected a church on land donated to them by Marco Ziani, son of Doge Pietro Ziani. Construction of the current building commenced in 1534, according to plans by Sansovino (1486-1570). The main façade with its crowning pediment is designed by **Palladio** (1508-80). One of the highest in Venice, the *campanile* serves as a point of reference from the most distant corners of the city. According to the records, it echoes the bell-tower of St Mark's.

The church houses works by **Gioanni Battista Tiepolo** (1696-1770), **Veronese** (1528-88) and **Giovanni Bellini** (1432-1516).

The construction of the presbytery was commissioned by Doge Andrea Gritti (1523-38) who is buried here. At the sides stand the two majestic Gritti monuments, the composite columns are by Sansovino.

The church's most famous masterpiece is to be found in the south transept: a *Madonna and Child Enthroned*★ painted in 1450 by the monk Antonio da Negroonte. This archetypal late-Gothic iece recalls works by Vivarini in ts structural format, figure types nd decorative detail.

rom Campo San Francesco della 'igna take Calle San Francesco and hen, to the left, Calle de Te Deum. Continue south, crossing the canal or the first time to reach the ondamenta San Giorgio degli chiavoni.

ollow the Fondamenta dei Furni southwards to the **Church of an Antonin**, which was rebuilt y Baldassare Longhena (1598-682). Salizzada San Antonin leads nto **Campo Bandiera e Moro**. he heroes of the Risorgimento, \ttilio and Emilio Bandiera, were orn here and remembered in the ame of the square, together with)omenico Moro, another patriot vho was shot down with them.

■ San Giovanni in Bràgora★

The name of this church has several possible derivations: from the Greek *agorà* which means piazza, or from the dialect "bragolà" (market square) or "bragolare" (to fish). Vivaldi was baptised here in 1678. The current building, with its obvious brick façade, was erected in the late 15C.

The interior comprises a nave with a trussed ceiling and two aisles. Of particular interest are the *Madonna and Child* by **Alvise Vivarini** (c 1445-1505), the *Baptism of Christ*★★ by Cima da Conegliano (c 1459-c 1517), works by Palma il Giovane (1544-1628) and Paris Bordone (1500-71), *The Resurrection*★ by Alvise Vivarini (c 1445-1505) and the *Madonna and Child with St John and St Andrew*★ (1478) by Bartolomeo Vivarini (1432-c 1491). ■

San Giovanni in Bragora

R. Corbel/MICHELIN

SAN ROCCO★★★

■ Scuola Grande di San Rocco★★★

In 1564, a competition was launched for the decoration of the Salla dell'Albergo *(a small room on the first floor where the Chapter met)*. Several illustrious artists, including Paolo Veronese (1528-88), Andrea Schiavone (1503-63), Giuseppe Salviati (1520/25-75) and Federico Zuccari (1540-1609), submitted their drawings, but Tintoretto (1518-94) quickly completed a painted panel for the ceiling depicting *St Roch in Glory* and promptly donated his work as a gesture of his devotion. The work, irrespective of what admiration it drew, could not be refused – and so Tintoretto went on to furnish the entire Scuola with his paintings depicting scenes from the Old and New Testaments.

The Sala capitolare is superb. The central panel on the ceiling depicts *The Brazen Serpent*: Aaron brandishes his rod, foreshadowing another cross that presages the delivery from sin.

This is framed by two square panels depicting *Moses Striking the Rock*, swirling with movement like a vortex around the central biblical character, and *Manna Sent from Heaven*. On the side of the corridor leading from the Albergo Room is depicted *The Pool of Bethesda*. *The Temptation of Christ* boasts a splendid Lucifer that echoes images of Eve tempting Adam with the apple. On the wall opposite, the *Adoration of the Shepherds* is followed by the *Baptism*, in which the protagonist is the Divine light that throws the faces of Jesus and John the Baptist into shadow in the central section opposite *The*

The Venetian Scuole

Instituted during the Middle Ages, the scuole (schools) were lay guilds drawn from the middle classes which were active in all aspects of life, be it devotional, charitable or professional, until the fall of the Republic. Each school had its own patron saint and mariegola, a rule book of the guild. In the 15C the scuole were housed in magnificent palaces with their interiors decorated by famous artists.

The hunchback (gobbo) of the Rialto

Some of the statues in Venice, such as the Moors in Campo dei Mori, adopt rather curious poses and expressions. The 16C **"gobbo di Rialto"**, a hunchback who is bent double beneath his burden, patiently supports the stairs before the column from where the *comandador* would proclaim government decrees.

A. Zane/MICHELIN

scension, The Resurrection of Christ shows Christ seemingly bursting from the tomb as the two Marys walk in the morning light beyond; n The Resurrection of Lazarus, the ree behind the main figures is silhouetted against the pale light; in The Agony in the Garden, the hour of the day embues the scene with a faint reddish light. The focal point of perspective in The Last Supper is the bright halo hovering over the little figure of the Saviour. Unfortunately, little remains of the full glory that might have graced The Miracle of the Loaves and Fishes, which succumbed to damage over the years from the light of the windows.

San Pantalon

Cross the canal behind the Scuola and take Calle San Pantalon which leads into a square. Despite its unfinished façade (1668-86), this church recalls others in Venice such as San Marcuola and San Lorenzo.

Its main interest, however, is its interior ornamented with an undisputed masterpiece by Fumiani (1643-1710) comprising 60 canvas ceiling panels illustrating The Martyrdom and Glory of St Pantaleon★, executed between 1684 and 1704. The work is a tour de force of perspective, projecting the nave high into the sky. The presbytery decoration is by the same artist, often referred to as fumoso (meaning smoky) owing to his predilection for dark colours, so characteristic of a period tormented by ever-present death. The church accomodates works by Antonio Vivarini (c 1420-84), Veronese (1528-88) and Palma il Giovane (1548-1628).

Return to San Rocco to take Salizzada San Rocco and Calle Larga Prima to Campo San Tomà. To reach Goldoni's house, keep to the left side of the church and cross the bridge over Rio San Tomà.

■ Casa di Goldoni

It was in this *palazzo*, its fine, small courtyard complete with its well and staircase, that the famous playwright **Carlo Goldon**i (1707-93) was born. The house is now home to the International Institute for Theatrical Research and has one room set out as a small puppet theatre, housing works by Goldoni and Pietro Longhi.

To continue to Campo San Polo, the easiest way is just to follow the flow of people. Cross the bridge over Rio di San Polo and follow along the right side of the church.

■ San Polo

The façade of this 9C ancien church was rebuilt between th 14C and 15C. Now hemmed in b houses, the church preserves it main rose window and an ornat side door decorated with organi carving from the turn of the 14C as a testimony to the late-Gothi style. Subsequent restoration in th 19C has unfortunately destroye the harmony of the original.

The interior, vaulted with a ship keel roof, accommodates work by Tintoretto (1518-1594), Tie polo (1696-1770) and Verones (1528-1588). ■

Carlo Goldoni(1707-93)

Goldoni's father was a doctor who wished his son to follow in his footsteps but when, aged 13, the boy absconded from school to join a ship in Rimini that was carrying a troupe of actors to Chioggia, from where he went on to join his mother in Venice.

In 1743 Goldoni wrote the script for *La donna di Garbo*. In 1750 the provocative comedy playwright impudently waged a bet with his rival Pietro Chiari that in less than a year he could write 16 new comedies: in fact he wrote 17, including the splendid *La Bottega del Caffè (The Coffee Shop)*. The ingredients were simple: he used colloquial language for immediacy and formulated rounded characters based on observation of real life. *Arlecchino, Servitore di due Padroni (Servant of Two Masters), La Locandiera (The Innkeeper)* are all constructed according to the same format.

Goldoni in campo San Bartolomeo...

SAN GIORGIO DEGLI SCHIAVONI***

▉ Scuola di San Giorgio degli Schiavoni***

The *Cycle of St George* by **Vittore Carpaccio** (c 1465-1526) took the artist five years to complete (1502-07). It was moved downstairs in the 16C, to the intimate ground-floor, well-lit gallery, with its fine wooden ceiling, which provided an ideal location to best show off the paintings' warm colours.

St George and the Dragon catches the very moment when the knight attacks the dragon: the event is narrated pictorially with all the romance of heroic chivalry, a veritable *chanson de geste* on canvas. The noble bearing of the saint and his steed, the dignified composure of the emotional princess and the architectural precision of the composition are true to the idealised legend, but contrast sharply with the macabre portrayal of skulls and hideously mutilated bodies.

The Triumph of St George dramatically depicts the saint on the point of killing the wounded dragon: the exotic figures are set against a background of Renaissance architecture.

The group of musicians is also present in the next scene, *St George Baptising the Heathen King and Queen,* as witnesses to the solemnity of the occasion: this is tempered only by the timorous pose of the saint, who is shown full of hesitation. The rich details also seem charged with expression: note the animals and the turban lying on the steps. The pre-eminent significance given to the chivalry of St George may be due to the financial support given to the Scuola by the Knights of Rhodes.

St Tryphon Exorcising the Daughter of the Emperor Gordianus is a rare representation of the saint. It has been painted by Carpaccio and his assistants, but a master's touch is recognisable in the architectural details and the distinctive personalities of the figures.

In *St Jerome leading his Lion into a Monastery*, the depiction of the monks is nothing short of humorous as they flee from the lion that is more concerned with obediently following St Jerome. Panic is carefully conveyed in the dashing movement of the monks towards the left, right and up the stairs. The building in the background is the Scuola di San Rocco.

The Legend of St George

The legend of St George slaying the dragon seems to emerge late in the 12C, when popularised in the **Golden Legend:** a story possibly founded on the myth of Perseus killing the sea monster at Arsuf or Joppa.

The symbolism inherent in the valiant saint slaying the dragon and saving the virtuous princess was exploited by the Church as a parable about the Church being saved from the devil.

There is solemn tragedy in the *Funeral of St Jerome*. Set in the peaceful, ordered precinct of a monastery, the composition centres around the saint laid out on the floor, attended by monks.

St Augustine in his Study also alludes to the legend of St Jerome: the story tells of St Augustine wishing to address a letter on a matter of theology to St Jerome, who had already died: his divine presence appeared in St Augustine's study admonishing him for his presumption (a Venetian edition of the letter was published in 1485). The study is flooded with natural light that highlights every detail including the dog's bemusement, the scrolls and the little knobs. The quality of rendering and exquisite attention to the furnishings, especially the open door into a second room, are reminiscent of Flemish domestic interior painting. The facial traits of St Augustine are, in fact, those of Cardinal **Bessarion** (1402-72), a scholar of Greek Humanism.

■ La Pietà

The white façade with its broad pediment supported on columns finally added in 1906, is the distinguishing feature from afar of Santa Maria della Visitazione better known as "La Pietà" (the merciful one) after its hospice for abandoned children, dedicated in the 14C.

In the 18C, it was decided that the church should be designed as a concert hall, given that the orphans' education was orientated towards music – at one time under the inspired leadership of Antonio Vivaldi (1678-1741).

The internal structure is vaulted to optimise the acoustics: oval in shape, its atrium successfully nuffles sounds from Riva degli Schiavoni. The orchestra and the choir are positioned along the side walls. Music is also the theme of the superb frescoes on the ceiling by GB Tiepolo (1696-1770).

Continue down the right side of the church along Calle della Pietà and Calle Bosello. Turn left into Salizzada dei Greci and then left again at the canal.

San Giorgio dei Greci

The closed complex designed by Longhena (1598-1682) and distin-

guished from afar by its gently leaning tower comprises a 16C church and college buildings reserved for its Greek Orthodox community, and the icon museum.

A confraternity evolved to form the Scuola di San Niccolò; after the fall of Constantinople in 1453, its numbers increased remarkably. Since 1539, first Sante Lombardo (1504-60) and then Giannantonio Chiona (active in Venice 1548-54) were charged with the church's expansion. The long and narrow façade with its prominent pediment owes much to the influence of Sansovino. The cupola was added in 1571.

Inside, the great rectangular space is completely sealed by a magnificent **iconostasis*** embellished with holy figures against a gold background that screens off the apsed area beyond, reserved for the clergy. The walls are lined with wooden stalls for use by the congregation during the long Orthodox rituals.

Museo di Icone Bizantine-post-bizantine – This museum houses a rich collection of Byzantine and post-Byzantine icons and paintings portraying various religious subjects that range from episodes from the Life of Christ (Christ with John the Baptist, the great 17C icon), the Saints, the Virgin, the Tree of Jesse, exquisite illuminated manuscripts and religious artefacts. ∎

AROUND THE MAIN CHURCHES

I FRARI★★★

■ The church

This great church – whose name is derived from the abbreviation of Fra*(ti Mino)*ri – has often been compared with the Church of Santi Giovanni e Paolo because of its sheer scale and style.

Monumental in stature, flanked by the second tallest campanile (70m/229ft 6in) after St Mark's, this building is massive yet articulated with fine architectural detail.

Santa Maria Gloriosa dei Frari – the church's full title – is in the form of a Latin cross. The nave is divided from the aisles by 12 huge cylindrical piers which soar up to the criss-cross of transverse and longitudinal timber beams that underpin the quadripartite vaults. The red and white floor tiles are from Verona.

Inside the church, note the Madonna di Ca'Pesaro Chapel, dominated by Titian's altarpiece, the 15C choir stalls, by Marco Cozzi da Vicenza, comprising 124 decorated stalls, and **Titian's** *Assumption of the Virgin*, which was commissioned by the Franciscans in 1516. This major work – the first religious subject undertaken by the painter – caused the friars some consternation because of its unorthodox iconography: Mary at that time was more usually represented in prayer, with an expression of divine rapture. Instead of restful contemplation, the crowded painting shows the Apostles disturbed by the mystery of this supernatural event; *putti* and winged angels singing and playing music, emphasise the upward movement of the composition, as the (nervous) Virgin looking ever upwards towards God the Father is received in the Kingdom of Heaven in a triumph of light and colour.

The sacristy houses the splendid Triptych by **Giovanni Bellini** (c 1426-1516), which exudes sweetness: the gentle expression of the Virgin as she turns to the angels who play the lute and flute and the serene air of the figures of St Nicholas, St Peter, St Mark and St Benedict *(from left to right)*.

Opposite is a lunette (1339) by Paolo Veneziano that was designed to be set above the Byzantine sarcophagus of **Doge Francesco Dandolo** (1329-39) in the adjacent Sala del Capitolo, the Capitolo being the periodic assembly of religious orders.

Titian's Mausoleum, hewn in marble from Carrara, was executed during the decade 1842-52. **Titian**, who died of the plague in

576, was buried in the Frari in accordance with his wishes, but by the end of the 16C all traces of his body had disappeared. The artist is depicted between the Nature of the Universe and the Genius of Knowledge.

Cross the canal in front of the church and turn left to Campo San Stin. Then take Calle del Tabacco and Calle dell'Olio as far as Campiello della Scuola.

■ Scuola di San Giovanni Evangelista

The elegant Renaissance iconostasis, with its crisply carved decoration, overlooked by the eagle of St John crouching in a lunette, was designed by Lombardo (1481). The elegant double stairway inside, lit with large arched windows, was built by Codussi (c 1440-1504).

Various craftsmen are responsible for the decoration on the ceiling and the walls, including Jacopo Guarana (1720-1808), Gaspare Diziani (1689-1767), Jacopo Marieschi (1711-94), Giandomenico Tiepolo (1727-1804), Domenico Tintoretto (c 1560-1635) and Pietro Longhi (1702-85).

Continue straight on as far as the Grand Canal, to come out opposite Santa Lucia Station. Turn right along the water's edge, where stands the church of San Simeon Piccolo. At Ponte degli Scalzi, turn right and then left into Calle Bergami.

■ San Simeon Grando

So-called to distinguish it from the Church of San Simeon Piccolo, the church is also known as San Simeon Profeta.

I Frari belltower

R. Corbel/MICHELIN

Although its origins go back as far as 967, the building has undergone considerable remodelling, particularly in the 18C. Although the ornamentation is generally heavy, there is an exquisite *Last Supper* by Tintoretto (1518-94).

Calle Larga dei Barbi, behind the church, leads into Campo Nazario Sauro. From here continue on to Campo San Giacomo dall'Orio, an open, often lonely space, and down Ruga Bella or the parallel Ruga Vecchia, which comes out directly in front of another church.

The altana is a veranda built on a tiled roof where typical Venetian chimneys project; they were immortalised by Carpaccio in his paintings. For ever short of space, the Venetians have made clever use of their rooftops by installing these charming terraces to increase their living area.

■ San Giacomo dall'Orio★

The church was founded in 976 but most of its present fabric dates from 1225. Its position and structure recall those of the Church of Santa Maria Formosa.

The bell-tower, erected in the 12C or 13C, is reminiscent of that on Torcello. The three apses date back to different periods: the left to the 16C, the central apse to the 13C and the right one to the 17C. The transept frontage dates from around the 14C.

Inside, it is perhaps the Gothic lacunar ceiling, shaped like an inverted ship's hull, that is most striking. The nave is divided from its aisles by five baseless columns

T. Zane-MICHELIN

down each side, the fourth marking the division of the transept. The unusual stoop for the holy water is made of cipolin (onion) marble from Anatolia. The church houses works by Palma il Giovane (1548-1628), Francesco Bassano (1549-1592) and Veronese.

In the arch of the vaulting, above the presbytery, is a wooden *Crucifix* attributed to Paolo Veneziano (c 1290-1362). The altarpiece, by Lorenzo Lotto (c 1480-1557), depicts the *Madonna and Saints*.

On the left wall of the left apsidal chapel are a pair of fine organ doors (1532), attributed to Schiavone.

To get to Campo San Giovanni Decollato and the church of the same name (Zan Degolà in Venetian), take Calle Larga and branch left down Calle dello Spezier.

■ San Zan Degolà

This church can trace its origins back to 1007, when the first parish church was built. The terracotta façade is early 18C. A rose window is the main feature of the central section of the three-tier facade, framed by pilasters supporting a triangular tympanum. The relief on the right wall retells the story of John's decapitation.

As with the façade, a harmonious simplicity pervades the interior: the three aisles are separated by four columns of Greek marble with 11C Byzantine capitals. The ceiling takes the form of an inverted ship's hull. ■

S. ZANIPÒLO ★★

Just one look at the square and the activities that seem to go on here – appearing little changed through the ages if compared with Canaletto's painting of *Campo Santi Giovanni e Paolo* – serves to justify its former name, *Campo delle Maravege* (Marvels).

The name *Zanipòlo* is a contraction of the names John and Paul in dialect, the two saints to whom the square is dedicated. Every one of its constituent elements contributes to the solemn vastness of the whole: the imposing basilica, the deceptive perspectives of the Scuola Grande di San Marco, the bridge over the Rio dei Mendicanti, the great "angular" space, relieved only by a well-head, and

the **equestrian monument t** **Bartolomeo Colleoni**, by Verroc chio (1435-1488).

■ Basilica dei Santi Giovanni e Paolo (San Zanipòlo) ★★

The church was founded by Do minican friars late in the 13C. I is reminiscent both in style (brick and size of the Frari. It is, in fact the largest church in Venice, bein 101m/330ft long, 46m/151ft wide at the cross and 55m/180ft tal to the top of the dome. Its particularly solemn atmosphere may in part be inherited from a time when it served to hold the doges obsequies and burial.

On either side of the main portal designed by Bartolomeo Bon (recorded 1441-64), are the two sar-

N. Bosques-MICHELIN

Streets, squares and picturesque corners bearing dialect names have ancient and unusual derivations. The churches dedicated to two saints, such as "Giovanni e Paolo" and "Gervasio e Protasio", are given a single name, an abbreviation in local dialect (Zanipòlo and Protaso). Other saints are also referred to by their "Venetian name": San Stae is the contraction of San Eustachio, and San Stin, of San Stefanino.

cophagi, inset in the Gothic arches, of the Doges Jacopo (1229-49) and Lorenzo (1268-75) Tiepolo.

The most striking element here is the architecture of the interior, with its well-lit lofty nave. Built in the form of a Latin cross, the church has three aisles and five apses. As in the Church of the Frari, huge columns carry great beams which support the arches and the cross vaults. The internal façade commemorates the Mocenigo Doges.

San Zanipòlo is lit by the brightly coloured stained-glass windows in the right transept. The panels are based upon cartoons by Bartolomeo Vivarini, Cima da Conegliano (c 1459-1517) and Girolamo Mocetto (c 1448-1531).

Of particular interest is the central apse and its funerary monuments: an exquisite *Virgin and Child* by Nino Pisano and apprentices, dedicated to the Doge Marco Corner (1365-68), is followed by the sepulchre of Doge Andrea Vendramin (1476-78), a majestic work by Tullio Lombardo ornamented with Classical medallions, the monument to Doge Michele Morosini (1382) from the workshops of Dalle Masegne) and the works of Veronese (1528-1588) in the **Cappella del Rosario** (Chapel of the Rosary or Lepanto Chapel).

■ Scuola Grande di San Marco★

This ancient Scuola, founded in 1260, was transferred here from its original seat in Santa Croce in 1438. Destroyed in the fire of 1485, its reconstruction was entrusted to Pietro Lombardo (1435-1515) and his sons, before being completed by Lombardo's arch rival, Mauro Codussi (c 1440-1504), who was responsible for the crowning section of the façade. At ground level, the façade boasts an effective series of *trompe l'oeil* panels; two bold lions guard the left entrance and, to their right, two groups of figures (by the Lombardo sons) crowd around St

Mark healing and baptising Anianus, a cobbler from Alexandria. At roof level, semicircular pediments and ornate statuary crown the elaborate frontage.

Follow Calle Larga Gallina to Campo Santa Maria Nova.

■ Santa Maria dei Miracoli★

This exquisite church, positioned on the edge of a canal overlooking the small Campo dei Miracoli, recalls the distinctive nature of 14C Tuscan design both in terms of its crisply carved architectural ornament and its marble detailing. The church is the work of Lombardo (1435-1515), erected to house a miracle-working image of the Madonna by Nicolò di Pietro (1409). The interior, especially the barrel vault, resembles a casket. Prophets and patriarchs are depicted in the 50 compartments of the coffered ceiling (best appreciated with the mirror provided for this purpose).

A flight of steps provides access to the elevated tribune, framed by a balustrade and ornamented with statues by Tullio Lombardo (active in Venice c 1455-1532). The painting by Nicolò di Pietro stands at the main altar.

Cross the bridge into Campiello Santa Maria Nova, pass before San Cancian and proceed straight on. Take Calle del Manganer in Campiello Cason which leads to the back of the Church of Santi Apostoli. Behind the church, take Rio Terà dei Santi Apostoli and carry straight on. The walk to the vast Campo dei Gesuiti will reveal secluded corners of Venice that are typical of the Cannaregio sestiere.

■ Gesuiti★

The present building was erected between 1715 and 1729 on the site of the ancient Church of Santa Maria dei Crociferi (1150).

The true originality of the building is reinforced on entering: the realism of the white marble curtain, inlaid with green, is so effective as to deceive one into believing in the ample drapes in the pulpit and the folds of carpet tumbling down from the high altar.

Detail of the well in Campo di SS Giovanni e Paolo

The sumptuous effect is enhanced by the white and gold stucco of the ceiling, the two central sections of which are by Francesco Fontebasso (1709-69).

Over the first altar on the left sits *The Martyrdom of St Lawrence* by Titian (1490-1576); in the left transept is the *Assumption of the Virgin* by Tintoretto (1518-94).

In the sacristy is a cycle of paintings by Palma il Giovane (1548-1628).

The Oratorio dei Crociferi is grouped around Campo dei Gesuiti.

From the Fondamenta Nuove take the vaporetto for the island of San Michele, where Venetians and many of her famous visitors have chosen to be buried.

■ San Michele in Isola

the great white church, designed by Codussi (c 1440-1504), the first Renaissance church in Venice. Its simple façade betrays the ordered structure of the interior: crowned like the Church of San Zaccaria and rusticated on the ground floor like the Palazzo Ruccellai and Palazzo Medici in Florence. Codussi purposefully avoids perfect symmetry and strict geometry by adapting the semicircular upper section.

Cimitero – Here lie Ezra Pound (1885-1972), Stravinsky (1882-1971), Diaghilev (1872-1929), since June 1997 Joseph Brodsky (1940-1996), Luigi Nono (1924-1990) and the great Goldoni actor Cesco Baseggio (1897-1971). ■

LA SALUTE★★

■ Santa Maria della Salute★★

It is surely one of the most important and obvious points of reference on the skyline of Venice. It is also very dear to the Venetians: in 1630, when their city was racked by plague, they pledged a solemn vow to erect a church once the epidemic subsided.

Their prayers were answered and, in 1631, **Baldassare Longhena** (1598-1682) was granted leave to develop his project. This impressive basilica is rendered all the more majestic by its magnificent flight of stairs up to the entrance. Dominated by the towering central dome, the great round volume emerges from an octagonal base:

a geometric shape that radiates t◦ eight façades.

An integral part in the design fabri◦ of this distinctive and universall◦ famous church is its modillion◦ and concentric volutes (known a◦ *orrechioni* – big ears).

At the apex of the overall compo◦ sition is a figure of the Madonn◦ clutching the baton of the *Capi◦ tana de Mar* (Captain-Generalshi◦ of the Sea), poised above th◦ balustraded lantern. On the lesse◦ dome stands St Mark, flanked by the weathervanes of the two cam◦ panili beyond, marking the far en◦ of the church.

The interior space is dictated by the main cupola, with the central area opening out into six chapels◦

La Salute and the Dogana

As if to concentrate the power of design, the polychrome marble floor converges on a central circle of five roses which, together with the other roses of the wider circle, suggest the idea of a rosary.

Note the *Descent of the Holy Spirit,* painted by Titian (1490-1576) in 1555.

At the high altar is a 12C icon, the *Madonna della Salute,* also referred to as *Mesopanditissa* because it came from a place of the same name in Candia (Crete). In the sacristy hangs a *Wedding at Cana* by Tintoretto in which the artist has included himself as the first Apostle on the left.

■ La Dogana

Further along the Fondamenta Dogana, with its very evocative view over St Mark's Basin, is the **Dogana da Mar**. Dating back to the 15C, it originally served as the customs point for goods arriving by sea: a Dogana di Terra on the fondamenta del Vin in the Rialto district, served as the equivalent for imports brought by land. The building's present appearance dates from the 17C. Fashioned to ressemble a ship's hull, a statue of *Fortune* towers over a golden globe supported by two atlantes.

■ Le Zattere★

A walk along these *fondamente* provides a thrilling view that might be expected from a long balcony with a perfect prospect over the Giudecca Canal, a rougher stretch of water than the Grand Canal, to the island of the Giudecca itself on the other side. Although the panorama here is less illustrious than the city it overlooks, the majestic buildings of the Giudecca have their own stories to tell: from the Mulino Stucky to the Redentore, combined with that of the Zitelle, these provide the most exuberant expressions of religious fervour in Venice.

The Feast of the Redeemer

It is still held on the third Sunday in July, perpetuating the tradition started by Doge Alvise Mocenigo. A bridge of boats across the Giudecca Canal used to be assembled to enable the procession to reach the island and allow free access to the faithful. In the evening of the preceding Saturday, a fireworks display would illuminate the sky and the lagoon with sparkling lights, bewitching the animated audience of Venetians and tourists gathered on the Riva degli Schiavoni.

The name Zattere was coined from one function served by the *fondamenta* in the 17C: its transportation of wood on rafts or *zattere*.

Take Calle della Scuola and proceed straight on to the entrance of the beautiful, if ill-famed, Palazzo Dario. Turn left in the direction of Palazzo Venier dei Leoni.

■ Collezione Peggy Guggenheim★★

The collection is housed in the incomplete **Palazzo Venier dei Leoni** (1749), which was designed by Lorenzo Boschetti, the architect of the Church of St Barnabas. The entrance is through the peaceful garden, in the shade of whose surroun- ding wall are two stones that mark the final resting places of Peggy Guggenheim herself and her "beloved babies" – her dogs. The niece of the American industrialist Solomon R Guggenheim, who instigated the museum of the same name in the famous spiral

building by Frank Lloyd Wright (1869-1959) in New York, Peggy Guggenheim built up her Venice collection between 1938 and 1979. She acquired the *palazzo* after the Second World War and lived there until her death, when according to her express wishes both the *palazzo* and the collection it housed were handed over to the Solomon Guggenheim Foundation. Like its counterpart in New York, the museum is arranged themati-cally, displaying parallel collections of Abstract and Surrealist works by the same artists. The collec-tion, which is particularly strong in Surrealist art, contains works by Braque, Picasso, Mondrian, Boc-cioni, Brancusi, Kandinsky, Chagall: *The Rain*; Balla: *Abstract Speed+Noise*; Severini: *Sea = Ballerina*; Mirò, De Chirico: *The Red Tower*; Max Ernst, Klee, Magritte: *Empire of Light*; Dali, Pollock, Calder: *Mobile*; Vasarely and Moore. Among the most nota-ble individual compositions are the 23 sculptures designed by Picasso nd executed by Egidio Costantini 1964). Outside, the sculpture that tands guard over the Grand Canal *The Angel of the City* by Marino Marini.

La Giudecca

t one time dotted with the villas of wealthy Venetian nobles, he prestigious Cipriani Hotel is he only one left to perpetuate he luxurious past of this island. Nowadays it is a haven for visitors wishing to take in the island's relaxed and peaceful atmosphere, if only for an hour or so, and the contrasting views of Venice extending beyond the canal.

Le Zitelle – The **Church of Santa Maria della Presentazione** was designed by Palladio (1508-80). The name *Zitelle* was coined from a reference to the girls accommodated in the adjoining hospice that forms part of the façade.

Il Redentore* – Like the Church of La Salute, the Redentore was built as a result of a motion carried by the Senate. With Venice decimated by the plague which had been raging for more than a year, **Doge Alvise Mocenigo** proposed (1576) that a new church should be dedicated to the Redeemer, and every year thereafter honoured by a solemn procession.

Palladio (1508-80) sought to make it fulfil its votive function over and above all else. Its longitudinal axis, which may only be fully appreciated inside, was necessary for the long procession of clergy and dignitaries to be accommodated. The flat, rigorously Classical façade is set up and back from a great flight of steps imaginatively inspired by biblical descriptions of the Temple in Jerusalem. This idealised view of the Catholic Church accommodating a modern, classically ordered building was also to determine the setting for the *Presentation of Mary at the Temple* by **Titian** (1490-1576) at the Accademia, as well as the version by Tintoretto (1518-94) at the Church of the Madonna dell'Orto.

Sant'Eufemia – This is the oldest church on the island, its origins dating back to the 9C. The late 16C *portico* on the left side, facing onto the Giudecca Canal, is from another church, now destroyed.

Still graced with the 11C Veneto-Byzantine capitals, the interior houses the colourful *San Rocco and the Angel* by **Bartolomeo Vivarini** (c 1432-91) *(first altar, right aisle)* and the frescoed ceiling is by Giambattista Canal (1745-1825).

Mulino Stucky – This prepossessing but rather awkward construction – which would perhaps be more at home in Dickens' London – is the work of late-19C German architects. ∎

SANTO STEFANO

This is perhaps one of the most elegant squares in the city. Dominated by a church in which concerts are regularly given, this lively meeting place is further animated by a news stand and *gelaterie* (ice-cream shops). Bustlingly busy during the day as people make their way between the Accademia Bridge and Calle dello Spezièr, it provides the perfect venue for an early evening stroll or *passeggiata*, when it takes on a magical air, caught in silence, yet populated by the lights of the *palazzi* and a purplish hue from the street lamps. Towering over the square is a monument (1882) to **Niccolò Tommaseo**.

■ Santo Stefano★

Only one side of the Church of St Stephen faces onto the square of the same name, allowing its fine brick frontage to go almost unnoticed, giving, as it does, onto a constrictingly narrow alleyway. Clearly Gothic in style, the church comprises a central vaulted nave flanked by lower side bays. The 15C portal is by Bartolomeo Bon (known 1441-64); note the particularly attractive suggestion of movement in the acanthus leaves. The elegant sculptures are crowned by the figure of God blessing an angel. The pinnacle down the side, lancet windows an rose all contribute to the poise the Gothic whole.

Construction of St Stephen's an the adjacent convent was initiate in the latter half of the 13C; th church, however, was modified an embellished in the 15C.

The campanile (60m/196ft 10i high) is one of the most famou in Venice. It is constructed in bric with a cornice in Istrian ston leading up to an octagonal spir Like other bell-towers in the cit it boasts its own story. Building o the 15C lower section was re sumed in 1544; when it collapse in 1585, it was the new masonr that crumbled, hit by lightning s violent that the bells melted. Fur ther damage incurred by subsid ence between the 17C and 18C has left the tower leaning at a angle like all the others.

The nave rises high above the aisles, vaulted by a fine woode ceiling shaped like an inverted ship's hull that was actually crafte by shipbuilders. Geometrical de signs relieve the red brick walls Like so many other churches i Venice, St Stephen's is a pantheon to the glory of the city (the tombs of **Giovanni Gabrieli** and **Franc esco Morosini**, the Peloponnesian

3. Longhena's monument to Bartolomeo d'Alviano). In the sacristy hang three works by Tintoretto. From the nearby Campo San Maurizio, continue as far as San Marco. Take the *calle Larga XXII Marzo*, which leads to the church of San Moisè.

San Moisè

Undoubtedly, the most striking feature of the church is its façade: built by Longhena's pupil Alessandro Tremignon in the 17C with the help of the Flemish artist Meyring, a disciple of Bernini, it is the epitome of excess. Ruskin (1819-1900) regarded the Church of San Moisé and Santa Maria Zobenigo as *"among the most remarkable in Venice for their manifestation of insolent atheism"*. The slating comments celebrate the vainglorious egos of the commissioning patrons, the Fini family. The interior is also Baroque. Here, Tintoretto's *Christ Washing his Disciples' Feet* is displayed.

From Calle Larga XXII Marzo, it is an easy walk to Campo San Fantin.

La Fenice★

The opera house and music-theatre, situated in a secluded and picturesque little square, was inaugurated in 1792. Construction was initiated by **Giannantonio Selva** (1751-1819), a friend of Canova, who was awarded the commission by winning a competition. Almost completely destroyed by fire in 1836, it was rebuilt and renamed La Fenice (The Phoenix) in honour of its emergence from the ashes, only to go up in flames for a second time in 1996. It has since been reconstructed to the original design.

Famous works which have been performed for the first time in the Fenice include *Tancredi* (1813), *Sigismondo* (1814) and *Semiramide* (1823) by Gioachino Rossini, and *Ernani* (1844), *Attila* (1846), *Rigoletto* (1851), *La Traviata* (1853) and *Simon Boccanegra* (1857) by Giuseppe Verdi.

Neo-Classical in style, La Fenice has two façades and two entrances, including one overlooking the canal. It is not difficult to imagine the difficulties posed by the spatial requirements of the auditorium, which is much bigger than the apparently narrow façade, a problem overcome by means of an ingenious series of stairways.

■ **San Fantin**

The Renaissance church wa begun by Scarpagnino (active i Venice between 1505 and 1549 and completed by San sovino (1486-70) Inside, ther

The Bovolo
Staircase

re two works by Palma il Giovane (1544-1628).

Walk along the west side of the Ateneo Veneto and continue along Calle della Mandola. Turn right into Campo Manin. To reach the peaceful square that houses the Palazzo Contarini del Bovolo, take the calle to the left of the stationers and turn right after the bend.

Scala del Bovolo*

The **Bovolo Staircase** is all the more impressive situated as it is off a tiny, peaceful courtyard overlooked by private houses. The delicate spiral staircase (*bovolo* in Venetian dialect), which seems to harmonise with a composite style drawn from both Gothic and Renaissance styles, is attributed to Giovanni Candi, who died in 1506.

From the top extends a lovely, yet disorientating, **view**★★ over the Venetian rooftops: churches may be identified by their bell-towers, although the height and the distance may tax the most discerning topographer.

Continue towards campo San Luca. Further along Calle del Teatro is the Goldoni Theatre. The reflection of the campanile of St Mark's in the canal can be seen from the bridge.

■ San Salvador

The 7C Church of San Salvador would have been consecrated by Pope Alexander III during his visit to Venice to meet Barbarossa in 1177. Despite having been subjected to various phases of rebuilding, the 17C façade, designed by Giuseppe Sardi, survives with its cannon ball embedded in the masonry since 1849. The arch that opens on to the Mercerie is 16C. The main layout was designed by Spavento, a little-known architect, continued after his death in 1509 by Tullio Lombardo and Sansovino. Inside, three square bays are aligned to form a nave. Here, numerous works of art are displayed (Tiziano, Paris Bordone, Giovanni Bellini). ■

SAN ZACCARIA★★

■ San Zaccaria★★

This magnificent church is situated in a lively square behind Riva degli Schiavoni. Coming from Campo San Provolo, the square is reached through the marble High Gothic archway with a relief depicting the *Madonna Enthroned with Child and Saints*. Once inside this elegant square, along the left side runs a 15C arcade beyond which extend cloisters that once harboured the convent cemetery. On the right is the façade of the former convent church with its 13C campanile: note *(on the left)* one of those curious reprimands that one comes across in Venice: in this case, a polite invitation to behave oneself properly! An apt reminder, perhaps, addressed to visitors of the famous female convent visited by the doge every Easter Monday.

The original church, founded in the 9C, has been partly incorporated into the new church: the right aisle was created from the left aisle of the old church. The present church, dating from the 15C, was built by Gambello and completed, at his death, by Codussi.

The splendid white façade, with its three tiers of round-headed windows, niches and semicircular pediment seems to soar high above the neighbouring houses and can even be seen from the Doges' Palace, towering above the dense mass of roofs and *altane* (wooden roof terraces). Contrived from a variety of architectural styles, its tall Gothic proportions are cloaked in Renaissance detail. At ground level the lower section is set with square polychrome panels that run horizontally. Above this, a continuous frieze of shell-headed flat niches introduce a vertical element that is then carried through the upper sections, accented first with three windows, then two and finally by a single central oculus. Gently, the Gothic configuration of tall nave and side aisles cede to Codussi's more Classical idiom: projecting piers give way to free-standing paired columns that extend up to a cornice, crowned with free standing figures – far removed from the statue of *St Zaccarias* by Alessandro Vittoria (1525-1608) above the main door.

The stunning interior is literally covered in paintings, the most important of which is Giovanni Bellini's *Sacra Conversazione* (1505) over the second altar on the left, a work of extraordinary sensitivity and delicate colour harmonies.

ollow Salizzada San Provolo and roceed straight to the canal; turn eft for the Diocesan **Museum of Religious Art**, which houses paintings and sculptures, sacred objects and congregational banners from deconsecrated churches.

Alternatively, return to Campo anti Filippo e Giacomo and take Calle della Chiesa, turn left before he canal and follow the water's edge through Campiello Querini and onto Campo Santa Maria Formosa.

■ Santa Maria Formosa

The original 7C church built here was dedicated, according to legend, to St Magnus, to whom the Madonna appeared in the form of a beautiful, shapely *(formosa)* woman. It was rebuilt by Codussi between 1492 and 1504. The 17C campanile retains, above the entrance, a grimacing mask and its original pinnacle.

The Chapel of the Scuola dei Bombardieri (mortar founders), which contains a *San Barnaba and Saints* by Palma il Vecchio. In the first chapel on the right is a *Madonna of the Misericordia* by Bartolomeo Vivarini.

The Facade
of San Zaccaria

B. Juge-MICHELIN

E.Zane-MICHELIN

■ Fondazione Querini-Stampalia Onlus★

Housed in a modern building, this museum, which contains a library and occasionally hosts temporary exhibitions, is of particular interest to visitors seeking to imbibe the atmosphere of a Venice long disappeared, when life in the city was synonymous with art.

Works of art on display here include a clay model for a sculpture of *Letizia Ramolino Bonapart* by Antonio Canova, paintings b' Palma il Giovane , Luca Giordano Lo Schiavone, Palma il Vecchie *(Francesco Querini* and *Paola Priu.*

Mercerie★

The countless number of shops selling goods which gave rise to the name of the historic commercial street in Venice provide access between St Mark's and the Rialto. In the past, this was the route chosen by nobles to make some triumphal entry into the Piazza San Marco.

The Mercerie fall into three main sections: *Merceria dell'Orologio, di San Zulin* and *di San Salvador.* At Merceria dell'Orologio 149, there is a relief which records the event that set panic among the group of rebels led by Baiamonte Tiepolo, who disbanded when a stone mortar was dropped on a standard-bearer.

Querini) and Giambattista Tiepolo (*Procurator and Sea Captain Dolfin*). Particularly worthy of note are the **series of panels**★★ by **Pietro Longhi**, predominantly devoted to the sacraments and hunting; the *Scenes of Public Life in Venice*★★ by **Gabriele Bella**; and the evocative *Presentation of Jesus in the Temple* by Giovanni Bellini.

Everyday Venetian life of the period is well depicted in the paintings *The Boxing Match* after Antonio Stom and *The Frozen Lagoon by the Fondamenta Nuove* by an anonymous 18C Venetian painter.

Follow Calle delle bande as far as Campo della Guerra.

■ San Zulian

This is the first church encountered along Merceria di San Marco. The façade, cramped by adjacent buildings, is richly ornamented. Above the portal, Tommaso Rangone, the benefactor of the church, is portrayed by Sansovino. Note also the columns that frame the cartouches and the windows below pediments. Under the main tympanum is a typically Venetian feature, a *serliana* consisting of a window with three openings named after **Sebastiano Serlio**.

The church, founded in the 9C, was remodelled during the late Renaissance by Sansovino and Alessandro Vittoria. The interior includes works by Palma il Giovane and Veronese. ■

CANNAREGIO

Exploring the Cannaregio district offers a variety of pleasures. This tranquil and poetic *sestiere* of narrow alleyways and squares includes the typically Venetian Ghetto quarter, which is surprisingly unfrequented by tourists. The station and the lively Strada Nuova are also found in this *sestiere*. This is where each and everyone can formulate their own impression of Venice: another Thomas Mann could be inspired to write a novel depicting the city's fading decadence, a modern playwright with the panache of Goldoni might discover a limitless source of material for a lively performance in dialect

■ San Giovanni Grisostomo

Shoehorned between the houses into a rather narrow passageway is the simple yet remarkable reddish façade of the Church of St John Chrysostom. Founded in 1080 the church was given its current appearance by **Mauro Codussi** and his son Domenico, who completed the project at his father's death. The compact and

The sestieri

These are the six subdivisions of Venice: San Marco, Castello, Cannaregio, Santa Croce, San Polo and Dorsoduro. Place names are as distinctive as Venice's system of house numbers, which can reach remarkable heights (up to almost 7 000), as these refer to individually numbered addresses within the whole sestiere rather than to a particular street or square. Do not try to apply common sense or logic in finding even numbers on one side of the street and odd ones on the other! Streets, squares and picturesque corners bearing dialect names have ancient and unusual derivations. It is interesting to note that the Venetians are democratic even in the names they give their streets and squares, most of which recall traditional trades, food and legends, rather than famous citizens.

5562 ULTIMO NUMERO
DEL SESTIER
DE S. MARCO

N. Bosques-MICHELIN

A somewhat
confusing
numbering system

well-proportioned interior, dominated by a dome resting on four
piers, is in the form of a Greek
cross. The church houses works
by Giovanni Bellini, Sebastiano del
Piombo, Tullio Lombardo.

Continue straight on to the large but
crowded Campo Santi Apostoli.

Santi Apostoli

Only one side of the **Church of
All Saints**, rebuilt in the 16C and
restored in the 18C, gives onto
the square. The tall campanile, so
visible from afar, is here detached
from the church. It is a composite structure, comprising a stone
pedestal at ground level that soars
up to a belfry with three-arched
openings. Inside the rectangular
church nestles the 15C Corner
Chapel, attributed to Codussi ,
which contains the *Communion of
St Lucy* by Tiepolo.

To get to Campo della Misericordia,
head down the Strada Nuova, then
turn right when you reach the church
of San Felice. Further along the Fondamenta della Misericordia there is a
delightful square, Campo dell'Abbazia,
imbued with a dreamy atmosphere of
melancholy and abandon.

Continue under the porticoes of
the old abbey to the bridge over the
Rio dei Muri from where one of the
few active *squeri* is visible. Retrac-
ing one's steps, the Corte Vecchia
which heads off to the left leads to
a corner of Venice that reveals the
city's most genuine nature, one that
is sometimes masked by an ephem-
eral, contrived beauty. This perfect
viewpoint overlooks the Sacca della
Misericordia, a cove that is normally
buffeted by the wind, from where
the view stretches into the distance,
punctuated only by the Island of San
Michele, the tranquil cemetery on
the water.

Alongside the Rio della Madonna
dell'Orto stands a *palazzo* charac-
terized by a low relief featuring a
man pulling a camel. This is the Palazzo Mastelli del Cammello which
belonged to a family of merchants
from Morea in the Peloponnese
who settled in Venice in 1112. The
name Mastelli was coined after the
thousands of *mastelli* (buckets) of
gold *zecchini* or Venetian sequins
they were meant to own.

■ Madonna dell'Orto★: the Tintoretto church

The parish church enjoys a magnificent position overlooking a quiet square paved in a brick herringbone pattern. The richly ornamented façade, also in brick, betrays the various stages of construction and refurbishment from its foundation in the 14C, through early Gothic and Renaissance periods. Patronage was entrusted to the miracle-working Madonna dell'Orto (Our Lady of the Vegetable Patch!) when a statue of the Madonna and Child was found in a sculptor's garden. The bell-tower culminates in a conical brick dome.

The spacious interior accommodates several important works of art by Cima da Conegliano, Jacopo Palma il Vecchio, Daniel van den Dyck, Tintoretto whose burial place is marked by a slab in a chapel on the right. The main altarpiece depicting the *Annunciation* is by Palma il Giovane; in the apse vault are Tintoretto's *Virtues*.

From Campo dei Mori follow the fondamenta della Sensa, then take the calle del Capitello.

■ Sant'Alvise★

Like the Church of Madonna dell'Orto, the Church of St Alvis is situated in a secluded, albeit busier, square. The simple brick façade is pierced merely by a rose window and a portal under a delicate pro-

thyrum. The statue in the lunette i of St Louis of Anjou, who lived to wards the end of the 13C and wa named Alvise by the Venetians.

The 17C frescoes by Antonio Torr and Pietro Ricchi lend an evocative three-dimensional effect to the fla ceiling. The entrance area is over looked by the *barco,* the pensil choir stalls used by the nuns supported by columns with 15C capitals and Gothic buttresses.

On entering note the 15C tem pera panel paintings on the lef which were executed by a pupi of Lazzaro Bastiani. These depic the *Giant with Feet of Clay, Solomo and the Queen of Sheba, Tobias an the Angel, Rachel at the Well, Th Adoration of the Golden Calf, Th Revelation of Joseph, Joshua and th Fall of Jericho* and *The Poverty of Jo* The church also houses works b Tiepolo.

Turn back in Calle del Capitell and continue straight ahead.

■ Ghetto★★

This secret corner of the Can naregio sestiere is the ghetto *pa excellence,* being the first Jewis quarter to be differentiated a such in Western Europe. The ter which seems to testify to th barbarities endured by the Jewis community was originally coine from the word *geto* in Venetia dialect. This referred to a loca bombard or mortar foundry: th g, normally pronounced soft (as ir

George), was hardened by the first Jews who came from Germany. Visit the Jewish Museum and the synagogues.

Cross the Cannaregio Canal by the Ponte dei Tre Archi.

∎ San Giobbe

Work on the church dedicated to Job was initiated by Antonio Gambello in the second half of the 15C and completed by Pietro Lombardo. Its distinctive, plain façade is broken by a fine Renaissance portal, above which preside the statues of San Bernardino, Sant'Alvise and St Anthony. St Francis and Job appear in the low relief enclosed in the lunette.

The interior comprises a single nave, with side chapels to the left and altars to the right.

The vault of the second chapel on the left is glazed in majolica tiles from the Florentine Della Robbia workshops active between 1400 and 1500.

Before the entrance into the presbytery is the coat of arms of Doge Cristoforo Moro, who is buried alongside his wife Cristina Sanudo in the presbytery: their tombstone is typically Lombard in style. Note the three mulberries, the fruit of the *moro*, included in the coat of arms, a synonym that was not wasted on Shakespeare , who wrote about a Moor in *Othello*. Desdemona would have been based upon the first wife; interestingly, Othello gives a handkerchief embroidered with small berries to Desdemona. ∎

Enter the Ghetto by the bridge and the 'sotoportego'

E. Zane–MICHELIN

Other Sights in Venice

THE CHURCHES
OF THE RIALTO
AND CASTELLO

■ **Beyond the Rialto
Bridge**

San Giacomo di Rialto – This church is traditionally considered to be the oldest in Venice: according to one document – although of dubious authenticity – the city was born on 25 March 421 when three consuls arrived from Padua to establish a commercial seat at the Rialto, and this church, which is also referred to as San Giacometto, was built to celebrate the event. Its present appearance dates from the

The Biennale...

The 100-year history of this international exhibition of modern art is long and controversial. From its beginnings, in 1895, it caused an outcry by exhibiting a painting called *Il Supremo Convegno* by Giacomo Grosso, which was deemed to be in poor taste. The Impressionists were only «invited» much later as the organisers, up until 1912 at least, preferred art from Middle Europe rather than Paris. The exhibition has always been held in the Castello Gardens. One particularly spectacular inauguration was that of the Russian pavilion in 1914, which was celebrated with an Orthodox mass in the presence of the Grand Duchess. Since the 1930s, other artistic venues have proliferated to include the Festival of Music, the Poetry Conventions, the Exhibition of the Cinema, held on the Lido since 1937, and the Theatre Festival. Besides all the controversy, the usual organisational problems and the philosophical and political diatribes, the Biennale has stood its ground: *"The Biennale is one hundred years old and, in certain ways, it is showing its age»*, said the Mayor of Venice. It may well be, however, that its uncomfortable position in the "eye of the storm" ensures a restlessness that guarantees its vitality.

The Feast of San Pietro di Castello

In the last week in June, the wide open space is lit with coloured lights and covered with stalls serving typically Venetian wines and delicacies. On the Sunday evening, everyone takes part in a tombola.

IC, when it was rebuilt to accommodate local residents drawn to the market in the square.

The façade boasts several striking features, namely the clock (despite being a 1938 reproduction), the campanile, which houses the clock and the bells, and the 14C portico.

San Cassiano – Although the origins of this church are rooted in the 9C, it has been subjected to various attempts at restoration: its present appearance is largely the result of 17C remodelling. It houses works by Leandro Bassano, Palma il Giovane and Tintoretto.

■ In Castello...

Sant'Elena di Castello – Up until the 11C, the island was known as *cavana* (refuge), as it provided sheltered anchorages to boatmen and fishermen. Its present name is derived from the name of St Helen, mother of the Emperor Constantine, whose relics are still housed in the church and were brought to Venice in 1211, after the Fourth Crusade. The Gothic façade is dominated by its portal (1467).

San Pietro di Castello★ – Despite the fact that its fame has always been usurped by St Mark's, the Church of St Peter at Castello was regarded as the official cathedral of Venice up until 1807, when St Mark's was merely considered the doge's chapel.

It was erected in the 8C on the foundations of a church that dates back to 650. Reminiscent of the Redentore, the façade conforms to Palladian design. On the right is the former late-16C Patriarchal Palace. The nearby campanile, which leans to one side, was rebuilt by Mauro Codussi.

The 17C interior reflects the influence of Palladio. It contains works by Veronese, Luca Giordano, Marco Basaiti.

The very elaborate high altar is based on designs by Longhena.

The marble seat known as St Peter's Cathedra is from Antioch: note the unusual back adapted from an Arab-Muslim funerary stele, decorated with inscriptions from the Koran in Cufic script. ■

EXCURSIONS

THE ISLANDS

■ Burano★★

It takes about 45min to get from Fondamenta Nuove (line 12) to Burano, the most colourful of the islands. The last stretch of the journey is along the Mazzorbo Canal, which separates Burano from the island of Mazzorbo. The two islands are linked by a wooden bridge.

È l'isola più colorata della laguna. Sull'uscio delle case che hanno assorbito i colori dell'arcobaleno, le donne lavorano al tombolo.

■ Il Lido☆☆

The Lido is Venice's favourite seaside resort. This sophisticated and

It is easy to get to the Lido: hop onto line 1, 82 or N from Piazza San Marco and half an hour later you're there! From Santa Maria Elisabetta there is a bus to Piazzale Bucintoro, which leads to Lungomare Guglielmo Marconi. This area is home to some of the Lido's best hotels, with their colourful beach huts along the seafront, as well as to the Casino and the headquarters of the Cinema Festival.

now slightly decadent place also plays host to the Casino and the Venice International Film Festival.

■ Murano★★

To get to the island: Board line 12, 13, 41 or 42 at Fondamenta Nuove.

By the end of the 13C, the threat of devastating fire was constant in Venice with its wooden buildings and the Grand Council decided to move the glassworks away from the city to Murano. It became known as the glassmaking island and a museum, **Museo di Arte Vetraria★**, displays a unique collection of glassware. The furnaces, the shouts of the vendors coaxing visitors into the glassware shops, should not detract from the artistic atmosphere of the island. The apse of the fine basilica, **Santi Maria e Donato★★**, is a masterpiece of 12C Veneto-Byzantine art and the **mosaic floor★★** recalls that of St Mark's.

■ San Giorgio Maggiore★★

Take the lines 1 and 52.

The island fulfils almost any preconceptions visitors might have of Venice, as well as providing a

The Lido beach

first-rate view over the whole city, a particularly evocative panorama punctuated by churches that might be identified by their bell-towers, and which feature in the background of many a painting.

The restoration of the island to its former beauty is largely due to the **Cini Foundation** and the Benedictines, who, for more than 1 000 years, have faithfully preserved the original liturgical tradition and Gregorian chants of San Giorgio, assisted by the Salesians, who are active in all fields of education and guidance. No one lives on the Is-

The most colourful of the lagoon islands

R. Mattes-MICHELIN

land of San Giorgio besides these dedicated souls. There is nowhere to stay, nowhere to eat or drink, for such places would distract the spirit and attract an influx of indiscriminate visitors.

The bell-tower was given its present form by Scalfarotto in 1726. It offers the best possible **view***** over Venice. Jacopo Tintoretto painted the two paintings in the presbytery of *The Last Supper* and *The Gathering of Manna from Heaven*.

■ San Lazzaro degli Armeni**

Located near the Lido, it takes about 30min to get to the island of San Lazzaro degli Armeni on line 10 from Riva degli Schiavoni (San Zaccaria). Tours are scheduled to coincide with the vaporetto times – the talk begins on landing and continues through the monastery visit. Should you require more time on the island, catch the vaporetto that leaves at around 2pm and check for the departure time of the second return service.

This island was especially loved by Lord Byron, as he found the atmosphere lifted his ascetic spirit in times of melancholy. Today, it is no less evocative to visiting travellers who, on arrival by vaporetto, are greeted by charming Armenian monks. In the Monastery seek out the famous and valuable historical manuscripts that are a testament not only to the Armenian heritage but also to the kindly Mechitar monks who dedicate themselves to preserving the Armenian culture.

■ Torcello**

From Fondamenta Nuove, take the same line (12) that goes to Burano, which is only minutes away from Torcello

It is almost a ghost island where only the stones speak of its glorious past. In 639 The inhabitants of Altinum fleeing from the Lombards settled on the island and built a church. Torcello became a bishopric. The 10C witnessed the glorious ascent of Venice whose power extended over the lagoon, but an aura of gloom pervaded the island as malaria decimated the population.

In the Basilica di Santa Maria Assunta the most striking feature are the **ancient mosaics**** for their brilliance and quality. ■

Isola di San Giorgio

The Last Judgement

The Last Judgement is the main subject of the mosaics (13C-14C) at the back of the church. From the Crucifixion there follows the Descent into Limbo: Christ tramples over many keys and a devil reduced to miniature proportions while determinedly clutching Adam's hand. Behind is Eve, her hands covered for reasons of propriety; to the right stands John the Baptist, who may easily be recognised by his long hair and camel-hair shirt. Dominating the central section is the *Deisis*: Christ in glory enclosed within a mandorla, the aura of His divinity, surrounded by the symbols of the Passion. He is flanked by the Virgin and John the Baptist and by two angels. Two more angels support the mandorla, from which flows the river of fire down to hell. At the foot of the cross stand Adam and Eve with entreating expressions. The angels' trumpets recall the dead from the bowels of the sea monsters that devoured them (to the right may be seen the victims of the sea, represented as a female allegory with bracelets). Note the angel with the *rotulus* in his hand unravelling the sky and the stars that are destined to fall. Below the souls are being weighed by St Michael: he is working to safeguard the salvation of those who deserve to be protected from the demons that burden the scale with bags of sins. To the left are the saved; to the right the damned. It is here that the presumptuous are pushed aside: the seven devils portray the seven deadly sins which stem from arrogance. The main figure is Lucifer, who holds the Antichrist and is sitting on Leviathan, the sea monster described in the Book of Job whose breath sets burning coals ablaze. Below the various punishments are depicted in truly apocalyptic terms: the Proud (kings) are engulfed by fire with Epulonus perhaps asking for a little water; the Lecherous are devoured by the flames of passion; the Gluttons are naked and gnaw at their hands; the Angry are surrounded by water; all that remains of the Covetous are their skulls, their eye sockets filled with worms.

DIRECTORY

■ Visit ■

Visitors spending one day in Venice should take in Piazza San Marco. You would need another day or two to get round the Accademia, the *Scuole* (Schools) and the churches which house many of the city's treasures. Anyone who has the luxury of a week in Venice will get a real feel for the place strolling along the narrow streets and exploring the islands in the lagoon.

The hub of public life is Piazza San Marco (see below) where tourists and citizens sit on the terraces of the famous Florian and Quadri cafés. The Florian is the most celebrated of all the cafés in Venice; founded in 1720 it has received Byron, Goethe, George Sand, Musset and Wagner within its mirrored and allegory-painted walls.

The shops in St Mark's have sumptuous window displays of lace, jewellery, mirrors and the famous glassware from Murano. The Mercerie – shopping streets – lead to the Rialto Bridge.

On the far side of this are the displays of greengrocers' *(erberie)* and fishmongers' shops *(pescherie)*.

■ Getting About ■

It goes without saying that in Venice public transport uses only liquid roads. It is important to bear in mind that heavy traffic on the Grand Canal and the fact that stops do not always take one "door to door" mean that walking can sometimes be quicker. However, on arrival in the city, the very sight of the first bridge (Ponte degli Scalzi, opposite the station, is particularly steep) can be tiring for visitors carrying heavy luggage. Likewise, walking up and down bridges all day can put even the most energetic walker to the test.

Visitors will find that they will happily make use of the famous Venetian water-boats, the **vaporetti**.

Listed below are the two most convenient routes:

– **Line 1** stops at all stops along the Grand Canal. Terminates at the Lido after stopping at piazzale Roma, the station and San Marco.

– **Line 82** is faster than Line 1 as it makes fewer stops. Stops at Tronchetto, Piazzale Roma, the Giudecca, San Giorgio, San Marco and the Lido.

Anyone needing a taxi should make sure that the cab has a yellow strip which carries the black symbol (for the area code) and the number, and that the taximeter or tariff is clearly visible. The Italian Tourist Board recommends that in the event of a dispute over the price, take down the number of the taxi and the time, and, most important of all, get a receipt with details of the route and the price you paid for the trip.

Visitors are urged not to use the unauthorised mini cabs that hang around outside railway stations, airports and other waiting areas.

To call a taxi in Venice, dial:

Radio Taxi, ☎ 041 522 23 03, 72 31 12

Ferrovia, ☎ 041 71 62 86

Piazzale Roma (S. Chiara), ☎ 041 71 69 22

Rialto, ☎ 041 523 05 75, 72 31 12

S. Marco (Molo), ☎ 041 522 97 50

Lido, ☎ 041 526 00 59

Aeroporto (Marco Polo), ☎ 041 541 50 84

Visitors who opt to walk will be relieved to learn that as well as a choice of three bridges crossing the Grand Canal (Scalzi, Rialto, Accademia) they can be "ferried" across the canal in a gondola. This service is available at seven points along the Grand Canal (Station, S. Marcuola, S. Sofia, al Carbon, S. Tomà, S. Samuele, S. Maria del Giglio): it is a very rapid journey. Be careful to keep your balance!

Visitors who want to enjoy the full experience of a **gondola** ride must be prepared to spend a considerably more. The price can be divided among six people who can be accommodated in a gondola. A tour in a gondola by night is an unforgettable experience but incurs considerable costs. For more information contact the Istituzione per la Conservazione della Gondola e la Tutela del Gondoliere, ☎ 041 528 50 75.

for young visitors

For those who are lucky enough to be aged between 14 and 29, the *Rolling Venice* card offers a range of discounts on youth hostels, hotels, campsites, public transport, university canteens, restaurants, museums, the Biennale and various shops taking part in this scheme. Cards can be purchased with proof of identity at the following places:

at the ACTV ticket offices;

at San Marco, corte Contarina 1529 at the offices of the Assessorato alle politiche giovanili, ☎ 041 27 47 645;

in Santa Croce, corte Canal 659, at the Agenzia Arte e Storia, ☎ 041 52 49 232 ;

in San Polo, calle del Castelforte San Rocco 3101, at the Associazione Italiana Alberghi per la Gioventù, ☎ 041 52 04 414.

■ Where to Eat ■

Lunch or dinner in one of the trattorias is one of the pleasures of Venetian life. High up the list of things to try are the fish and seafood (in particular the squid, cuttlefish, eels and mussels), as well as *fegato alla veneziana* (calf's liver fried with onions). There are some excellent local wines to accompany these dishes including Valpolicella, Bardolino and Amarone (red) along with Soave and Prosecco (white).

⊖ Budget
⊖⊜ Moderate
⊖⊜⊟ Expensive

⊖ **Alla Patatina** – *San Polo 2741/A, Calle Saoneri* – ☏ *041 52 37 238* – *www.lapatatina.it* Pleasant 1950s-style establishment with a lively atmosphere. On offer at the bar are plenty of vegetable antipasti (including, of course, the delicious roast potatoes they do so well here) along with *polpette al sugo* (meatballs with sauce). Standard table service also available.

⊖ **Gam-Gam** – *Fondamenta Pescaria 1122* – ☏ *041 71 52 84* – *www.jewishvenice.org* – ✄ – *Book.* For anyone looking for something a little different or even a complete change of scene, you could try this rather pleasant Jewish restaurant. Modern, if austere decor. Strictly kosher food.

⊖ **S. Trovaso** – *1016, Dorsoduro* – ☏ *041 52 03 703* – *giorgiocassan@tin.it* – *Book.* This establishment is conveniently situated near the Accademia. It is always very crowded so remember to book! Good selection of dishes as well as pizzas.

⊖ **La Zucca** – *Sestiere S. Croce 1762* – ☏ *041 52 41 570* – *Book.* If you're in the mood for more varied and exotic dishes, prepared with a lightness of touch, this is the place to go. A simple trattoria, it offers a particularly good selection of vegetables dishes – the decor itself is a celebration of the pumpkin *(zucca)*!

⊖⊜ **Ai Frati** – *Fondamenta Venier 4 – 30141 Murano* – ☏ *041 73 66 94.* Founded as a wine shop in the mid-19C, it has since mutated into an eatery. For more than half a century now it has been serving good, authentic home cooking. The dining room is very pleasant but for a real treat try and get a table on the terrace overlooking the canal.

⊖⊜ **Al Mascaron** – *Calle Longa Santa Maria Formosa 5225* – ☏ *041 52 25 995* – ✄. This is arguably the most successful restaurant in Venice…and that is saying something. It is a very lively, noisy place and always busy. Excellent home cooking. Definitely one for the address book.

⊖⊜ **Trattoria Favorita** – *Via Francesco Duodo 33 – 30126 Venezia Lido* – ☏ *041 52 61 626.* What could be better after a long walk or a sunny day by the sea, than some delicious seafood or a traditionally cooked fish dish? Rustic-style ambience and tables outside. Very popular with the locals.

⊖⊜ **Alle Testiere** – *Calle del Mondo Novo 5801, Castello* – ☏ *041 52 27 220* – ▤ ✎ – *Book.* A small, informal establishment. The napkins might be made of paper but the cooking is a rather gastronomic affair. The menu, which focuses mostly on fish dishes, depends on what was on sale at the market that morning. A real treat for you (and your wallet!).

⊖⊜⊟ **Harry's Dolci** – *Fondamenta San Biagio 773, Giudecca* – ☏ *041 52 24 844* – ▤. Both restaurant and pasticceria, this is a little less expensive than its more famous sister establishment across the way. Stylistically it owes much to the Harry's tradition with diners seated close together in comfy chairs at low tables. Spectacular view from the large terrace overlooking the Canale della Giudecca.

■ Where to Stay ■

⊃ Budget
⊃⊖ Moderate
⊃⊖⊕ Expensive

⊃ **Istituto San Giuseppe** – *Ponte della Guerra 5402, Castello* – ☎ *041 52 25 352* – ✄ – *11 rm*

⊃ **Casa Caburlotto** – *Fondamenta Rizzi 316, S. Croce* – ☎ *041 71 08 77 – Fax 041 71 08 75* – ✄ – *30 rm*

⊃ **Casa Capitanio** – *S. Croce 561* – ☎ *041 52 03 099 – Fax 041 52 23 975* – ✄ – *12 rm*

⊃ **Casa Cardinal Piazza** – *Cannaregio 3539/A* – ☎ *041 72 13 88 – Fax 041 70 02 33* – ✄ – *24 rm*

⊃ **Casa Murialdo – Circolo ANSPI** – *Cannaregio 3512* – ☎ *041 71 99 33 – Fax 041 72 00 02* – ✄ – *12 rm*

⊃ **Domus Civica** – *S. Polo 3082* – ☎ *041 72 11 03 – Fax 041 52 27 139* – ✄ – *100 beds*

⊃ **Foresteria Valdese** – *Castello 5170* – ☎ *041 52 86 797 – Fax 041 24 16 238* – ✄ – *6 rm*

⊃ **Opera Pia Istituto Ciliota** – *Calle delle Muneghe 2976* – ☎ *041 52 04 888 – Fax 041 52 12 730* – ✄ – *39 rm*

⊃ **Patronato Salesiano Leone XIII** – *Castello 1281* – ☎ *041 24 03 611 – Fax 041 24 03 610* – ✄ – *15 rm*

⊃ **Santa Fosca** – *Cannaregio 2372* – ☎ *041 71 57 75 – Fax 041 71 57 75* – ✄ – *121 beds*

⊖ **Ostello della Giudecca** – *Fondamenta Zitelle 86, Isola della Giudecca* – ☎ *041 52 38 211 – Fax 041 52 35 689 – vehostel@tin.it* – ✄ – *260 beds*. An excellent base for exploring (by vaporetto!) one of the most fascinating cities in the world…and without burning a hole in your pocket. Marvellous situation – on the Giudecca, overlooking the lagoon and the city.

⊖ **Hotel Bernardi – Semenzato** – *Calle dell'Oca 4366 – Vaporetto Cà d'Oro* – ☎ *041 71 04 01 – Fax 041 71 08 17*. A no-frills hotel (stylewise the rooms leave a bit to be desired) but it is well situated (in a small street behind Campo S.S. Apostoli, near the Rialto bridge) in a less touristy part, although right at the heart, of the city.

⊖⊕ **Locanda Cà Foscari** – *Calle della Frescade 3887/B – Vaporetto San Tomà* – ☎ *041 71 04 01 – Fax 041 71 08 17 – valtersc@tin.it* – ✄ – *11 rm*. A very simple but pleasant establishment with light, airy rooms and a family atmosphere. Offers extremely good value for money – a very rare thing in Venice.

⊜⊜ **Hotel Locanda Fiorita** – *Campiello Novo 3457/A, San Marco* – ☏ *04 52 34 754 – Fax 041 52 28 043* – ▤ *– 10 rm.* A good little hotel house in a lovely old building. It is situated in one of the city's most attractive lit tle squares, just a stone's throw from the very famous Piazza S. Marco. The rooms are rather functional and the public areas could be better but who wants to stay in their room when there is the whole of Venice to explore?

⊜⊜ **Hotel Serenissima** – *Calle Goldoni 4486, San Marco* – ☏ *041 5. 00 011 – Fax 041 52 23 292.* This unpretentious hotel is ideally located between the Rialto Bridge and St Mark's Square. The rooms are simply furnished but tastefully decorated (some in Venetian style) and well kept One of the main attractions here is the staff who are very pleasant, creat ing a friendly, family atmosphere.

⊜⊜ **La Calcina** – *Fondamenta Zattere ai Gesuati 780, Dorsoduro – Vaporett Zattere* – ☏ *041 52 06 466 – Fax 041 52 27 045* – ▤. Only a photograph remains in the hallway of the «La Calcina» inn where Ruskin stayed in 1876, but this hotel, completely remodelled, stands on that very site. And it is as pleasant now as it was then; in the breakfast room as in the bedrooms on the roof terrace as on the waterside terrace. The fine location on the Grand Canal adds to its charm as does the light which floods in, a rarity in Venice's narrow streets.

⊜⊜⊛ **Hotel La Residenza** – *Campo Bandiera e Moro 3608, Castello* – ☏ *041 52 85 315 – Fax 041 52 38 859* – ▤. A stone's throw from Piazza San Marco is this lovely 16C palazzo which has been lovingly restored to its former glory – the perfect setting for a dream holiday. Features include 18C stuccowork, along with period light fittings and furnishings. The other main attraction is the wonderful view of the campo. Reasonably priced.

⊜⊜⊛ **Pensione Seguso** – *Zattere 779* – ☏ *041 52 86 858 – Fax 041 52 22 340.* Whether it is the wooden panelling or the round windows, but there is something rather pleasantly old-fashioned and Anglo-Saxon about this hotel. Previous visitors include Italo Calvino and Ezra Pound.

⊜⊜⊛ **Hotel Paganelli** – *Riva degli Schiavoni 4687, Castello* – ☏ *041 52 24 324 – Fax 041 52 39 267* – ▤. This family-run hotel overlooks the Bacino di San Marco. Some rooms (all decorated in the Venetian style) enjoy this view, others (in an adjoining building) look out onto Campo San Zaccaria

⊜⊜⊛ **Hotel Falier** – *Salizzata San Pantalon 130, Santa Croce* – ☏ *041 71 08 82 – Fax 041 52 06 554.* Close to I Frari but away from the bustling town centre, this hotel is a quiet haven of peace. Rustic-style decor with classic overtones. Charming little back garden where breakfast is served.

⊜⊜⊛ **Hotel Abbazia** – *Calle Priuli dei Cavalletti 68, Cannaregio* – ☏ *041 71 73 33 – Fax 041 71 79 49* – ▤. An ideal location for visitors wishing to stay near the station. This hotel once housed a Carmelite monastery and retains many of its original features including the pulpit in the entrance hall. Attentive, professional staff. The rooms are plain but spacious and there is a lovely garden.

Hotel Danieli – *Riva degli Schiavoni 4196, Castello* – ☎ *041 52 26 480* – *Fax 041 52 00 208* – 🖳 ✆. Possibly the most famous hotel in the world! For many the image conjured up by Venice is that of palaces in the mist, decadent shapes and colours blurred in the mind's eye with cinematic and literary associations. Walking into Palazzo Dandolo, the Hotel Danieli since 1822, is like walking into that imaginary portrait. The columns, staircase, open gallery and architectural embroidery are reminiscent of the decorative richness of King Ludwig's castle at Neuschwanstein in Bavaria.

■ Taking a break ■

Caffè Florian – *Piazza San Marco 55.* – ☎ *041 52 05 641* – *www.paginegialle.it/caffeflorian.* You can't go to Venice without experiencing the city's most famous café, named after its first proprietor Floriano Francesconi. With its elegant 18C salons, smart waiters and magnificent exterior it is a throw-back to its past even with all the hustle and bustle. Past habitués of renown have included the playwright Goldoni (1707-93) and the neo-Classical sculptor Canova (1757-1822). Also hosts musical soirées.

Caffè Quadri – *Piazza San Marco 120* – ☎ *041 52 22 105* – *quadri@quadrivenice.com* You will need a break from all that sightseeing so why not treat yourself to a top-quality cup of coffee? In the arcaded portico of the Procuratie Vecchie is the elegant Caffè Quadri, which was founded by Giorgio Quadri in 1775 and was one of the first cafés in Venice to serve Turkish coffee.

Devil's Forrest – *San Marco (Calle degli Stagneri) 5185* – *S. Giorgio degli Schiavoni.* – ☎ *041 52 00 623.* Beer, beer and more beer. You can even play darts here!

Harry's Bar – *San Marco (Calle Vallaresso) 1322* – *Piazza San Marco.* – ☎ *041 52 85 777.* Not far from the Piazza San Marco is the legendary Harry's Bar. Opened in 1931 by Giuseppe Cipriani, it boasts the writer Ernest Hemingway as one of its regulars. These days, it is popular with the locals and tourists alike who come and enjoy the elegant surroundings while sipping the house cocktail, a "Bellini", which is made with champagne and peach juice.

Marchini – *San Marco 2769* – *La Fenice* – *near Campo Santo Stefano, in the busy thoroughfare, Calle del Piovan, heading for San Marco.* – ☎ *041 52 29 109* – *www.golosessi.com* Elegant pasticceria with a very inviting window display!

Paolin – *Sestiere San Marco 3464* – *La Fenice.* – ☎ *04 15 22 07 10.* *Offers an imaginative selection of delicious ice creams (all made with milk of course). Flavours include* Tiramisù, Torrone (nougat) and Yogurt. For an even more luxurious experience there are a number of extras on offer including candied fruit, whipped cream, custard and there is even a liquorice/aniseed topping for the more adventurous.

Piero e Mauro – *Calle dei Fabbri 881* – *Piazza San Marco.* – ☎ *04 15 23 77 56.* Good selection of sandwiches, *crostini* (toasted bread snacks) and beers. The decor is fun too: the rather cramped room is decorated like the interior of a boat.

Rosa Salva – *San Marco (Marzaria San Salvator) 5020* – *La Fenice.* – ☎ *041 52 25 385.* You might have to stand up but it's worth it. They say this place serves the best cappuccino in Venice. Why not have a delicious pastry with it?

The Fiddler's Elbow – *Cannaregio (Corte dei Pali) 3847* – *Ca' D'Oro* – ☎ *041 52 39 930.* If you fancy an Irish coffee or a pint, how about a trip to this Irish pub?

■ Going out ■

Al Volto – *San Marco 4081* – *La Fenice* – very near *Campo Manin.* – ☎ *041 52 28 945.* With its collection of vintage wines, this wine bar is popular with serious wine buffs. Warm, welcoming atmosphere – can get very busy.

Il Paradiso perduto – *Cannaregio (Fondamenta della Misericordia) 2540* – *Ca' D'Oro* – ☎ *041 72 05 81.* An unusual establishment with live music, poetry readings and good food.

Linea d'Ombra – *Dorsoduro (Punta della Dogana) 19* – *La Salute.* – ☎ *041 52 85 259.* This rather elegant piano bar is situated round the corner from the Dogana del Mar, on the Zattere. Wonderful views of the Giudecca. Serves good cocktails.

■ Entertainment ■

Music and theatre have always formed an intrinsic part of the spirit of Venice. As well as the three major theatres, concerts and plays are also held in numerous churches such as the Pietà, the Frari, S. Stefano, all ideal concert halls. See the *Gazzettino* for all information on concerts and shows in the city.

Gran Teatro La Fenice – For information call ☎ 041 78 65 11.

Teatro Malibran – ☎ 041 7865 11.

Teatro Goldoni – Situated on the Calle del Teatro. Offers a rich season of plays and concerts. ☎ 041 24 02 011.

Teatro a l'Avogaria – Situated in Calle Avogaria, 1617 in the Dorsoduro quarter. ☎ 041 520 61 30.

Teatro Fondamenta Nuove – Situated on the Fondamenta Nuove, near the Sacca della Misericordia (Cannaregio 5013). Plays, concerts and dance. For information call ☎ 041 522 44 98.

INDEX